RHINE VALLEY
From Cologne to Mainz

By the staff of Editions Berlitz

Preface

A new kind of travel guide for the jet age—and one of an extensive series by Berlitz on the world's top tourist areas—this compact and colourful book is packed with all you need to know about the Rhine Valley.

Like our phrase books and dictionaries, this guide fits your pocket—in both size and price. It also aims to fit your travel needs:

- It concentrates on your specific destination—the Rhine Valley—not an entire country.

- It combines easy reading with fast facts: what to see and do, where to shop, what to eat.

- An authoritative A-to-Z "blueprint" fills the back of the book, giving clear-cut answers to all your questions, from "Where should we start our river cruise?" to "Where can I change money on the weekends?"—plus how to get there, when to go and what to budget for.

- Easy-to-read, full-colour maps pinpoint sights you'll want to see in the countryside and cities of the Rhine Valley.

In short, this handy guide will help you enjoy your visit to the Rhine Valley. From fairytale castles to the rock of the Lorelei, from the cathedral of Cologne to the celebrated Rhine wines, Berlitz tells you clearly and concisely what it's all about.

Let your travel agent help you choose a hotel. Let a restaurant guide help you find a good place to eat. But to decide "What should we do today?" travel with Berlitz.

Area specialist: Jack Altman
Photography: Monique Jacot
For their help in the preparation of this book, we wish to thank the German National Tourist Office of Zurich, in particular, Werner Pompl. We are also grateful to the KD German Rhine Line, the Tourist Office of Cologne and Lufthansa German Airlines for their considerable assistance.

Cartography: Falk-Verlag, Hamburg.

Contents

The Region and its People		6
A Brief History		12
Where to Go		29
	Cologne	33
	South to Koblenz	42
	Rhine Valley	51
Excursions	Mosel	67
	Heidelberg and Worms	76
	Düsseldorf	80
What to Do	Shopping	83
	Entertainment	87
	Sports	91
Wining and Dining		92
How to Get There and When to Go		101
Planning Your Budget		103
Blueprint for a Perfect Trip		104
Index		126

Maps: Rhineland pp. 30–31, Cologne p. 39, Bonn p. 42, Rhine Valley p. 52, Mainz p. 63.
Photos: Cover, Burg Pfalzgrafenstein; pp. 2–3, river view of Cologne and its cathedral.

How to use this guide
If time is short, look for items to visit which are printed in bold type, e.g. **Stolzenfels.** Those sights most highly recommended are not only given in bold type but also carry our traveller symbol, e.g. **Kloster Eberbach.**

The Region and its People

Mists and towering rocks, terraced vineyards and avenues of poplars, Gothic churches and ruined castles, the Rhineland assembles every poetic image dear to the romantic side of the German character. But it's also coal barges, express trains and juggernaut lorries, cement works and power plants. Rhinelanders settle down to their romantic dreams only after a hard day's work.

The river Rhine flows by six countries—Switzerland, Liechtenstein, Austria, France, Ger-

many and Holland—starting high in the Swiss Alps and running down to the North Sea at Rotterdam. But it's the stretch between Mainz and Cologne that offers this unique mixture of mysterious beauty and vigorous productive energy. Here, in the Rhineland proper, life for all its serious dedication to progress and prosperity seems somehow less rigid and tough than in many other parts of Germany. Its corners are nicely rounded.

Most unusual of all the half-timbered houses in Bernkastel-Kues, the top-heavy Spitzhaus.

The work gets done and well done, but the people always seem to have time to enjoy the pleasures of a smiling existence. After World War II, when West Germany (separated from Berlin) had to decide where to put its governmental capital, the future Chancellor Konrad Adenauer pushed successfully for Bonn on the Rhine. Not only for the political advantage of avoiding traditional socialist strongholds like Hamburg and Frankfurt, but also—as both his friends and his enemies said—so "der Alte" could continue to look after his beloved rose garden at nearby Rhöndorf.

Heartland of Germany the Rhineland may be, but it's scarcely typical of the popular image of German life. Certainly not as far as Bonn itself, that most paradoxical of capitals, is concerned. It's a town without the remotest notion of bustle seeking to govern a country where bustle is the philosophy of life. There are those who say that if Bonn had always been the nation's capital, the siesta would have been a German rather than a Spanish invention.

The Rhineland lies at the centre of a pious but never austere religious tradition where good Catholics take a secular, even pagan delight in the joys of the flesh. The great symbol of the Church's abiding authority is Cologne's gigantic, almost overpowering, twin-spired cathedral. And Mainz proudly points to its historic role in the Catholic Church, where for centuries it ranked second after Rome in Christendom's spiritual (and political) hierarchy. At the same time these two towns are the scene every year of Germany's most riotous, lusty, frolicking Carnivals, when wives put away their wedding rings and the husbands are not home to complain.

Cologne, long a commercial and cultural centre, has witnessed the nation's growth from earliest Roman times through medieval prosperity to its present state of comfortable stability. Mainz, with a distinguished intellectual tradition, has carried forward the legacy of Johannes Gutenberg's printing press, and its publishing houses and university add a refining touch to the "golden" city's robust sense of humour.

This cordial region has mastered the knack of making

Rhineland champion shot finds a cold glass of beer right on target.

8

the toughest ideas palatable. Koblenz sits at an elbow in the Rhine marked by that somewhat formidable Wilhelmian monument to German unity known as *Deutsches Eck* (German Corner). But it is also happily the point where the Mosel joins the Rhine, where the great white wines from both regions flow together—at separate tables, of course—with supporters for their rival qualities as fervent as any football fan. When you leave Koblenz, you tend to remember the hock rather than the Eck.

As delicious as the Rhine wines may be, the river's waters don't bear too close an inspection. Long before it reaches the mighty industrial Ruhr region, the Swiss city of Basel, the French factories be-

An unhurried ferry ride adds to the charm of the idyllic setting.

tween Kembs and Lauterbourg and the potassium mines at Mannheim-Ludwigshafen have done their dirtiest to the river flowing between Mainz and Cologne. But nobody ever sang about the Blue Rhine. The river's poets concentrated on the mythology rather than the quality of the water (though it was once clean enough for the babies of Mainz to be baptized in it). And when Heinrich Heine waxed lyrical about the Lorelei siren luring the Rhine sailors to their doom (see p. 58), it was the cliffs that sparkled golden in the evening sunlight, not the waters of the Rhine.

But after all, nobody really expects the Rhine to be limpid. Not even the fishermen who sit there dreamily on the river's banks, insistent that the perch and the pike they claim they catch are perfectly safe to eat.

For those who share the Germans' taste for forays into areas of nature still unspoilt by man and his industry, the Rhineland offers more than the river and its valley. There are the crater lakes of the vast Eifel mountain plateau between Bonn and the Mosel, the hills of the Hunsrück south of the Mosel, and then on the right bank of the Rhine the forests in the Taunus north of Wies-

baden. There you can indulge in that special German emotion—*Waldeinsamkeit*. One of those great untranslatable German words, it means approximately "the loneliness of the forest", but without any negative sense other than a certain wistful melancholy. One dictionary helplessly suggests "sylvan solitude", but don't bother to translate it. Just enter into the spirit and discover an important part of the Rhineland's mystery.

Such total immersion in nature, even if only for a day or so, will bring you closer to the region's heart. You'll realize that the Rhine Valley is not basically an industrial water route linking big cities from the Alps to the North Sea, but very distinctly a ribbon of quite conservative, mostly rural traditionalism. Hiking, camping, fishing and hunting are not just holiday sports for the true Rhinelander. They are a way of life.

You can sense this best in the small villages, especially south of Koblenz, in St. Goar, Oberwesel, Kaub, Bacharach, Oestrich and Eltville. Villages where they still observe old customs—the changes in the seasons, the arrival of spring, the wine-harvest and the autumn markets. Births, weddings **11** and funerals are celebrated with costume and ceremony, with an unabashed fidelity to a folklore that has died out in more self-conscious countries. Even sophisticated towns like Düsseldorf, Mainz, Cologne and Bonn will sport the masks of the Lenten Carnival and the grotesque lanterns of the November feast of St. Martin.

And once the wine starts flowing, the old folk songs come pouring out. Disco momentarily disappears. It's no surprise to learn that poet Clemens Brentano, who was one of the first to collect and write down the treasured folk songs, was born in Ehrenbreitstein, across the river from Koblenz.

Singing, dancing, clowning around, the Rhinelanders have a lust for life that doesn't need an official holiday as an excuse for a celebration. If there are enough friends gathered together by chance and enough wine to go round, there'll be a party. If you're lucky enough to be swept up into any of these impromptu festivities, be prepared to be the smiling victim of a practical joke or two. Rhinelanders are the acknowledged champions. They'll do almost anything short of throwing you in the Rhine. That would be no joke.

A Brief History

The Rhineland has a good claim to being the cradle of German civilization. It does seem more than a coincidence that the three major finds of prehistoric human remains in Germany were all found in the Rhine region.

Homo Heidelbergensis, as he is elegantly known, was a pithecanthropoid fellow living about 500,000 years ago. You can take a look at his jawbone when you visit Heidelberg. More famous is our old friend the Neanderthal Man, who died about 50,000 years ago. He is now on display at the Rheinisches Landesmuseum in Bonn (see p. 45) together with the Cro-Magnons of Oberkassel, the first couple to be unearthed. The small carved bone figures found with their remains suggest an early form of religious observance, a tradition that was to be a lasting feature of life in the Rhineland.

The river Rhine itself, taking its name from a Celtic word meaning roughly "current", was regarded by the Celts who inhabited the region around 1000–750 B.C. as the guardian of chastity, domestic honour and purity—in the days before municipal sewage.

As the climate grew cooler, most of the Celts moved west to settle on the left bank of the Rhine Valley while the Germans (another Celtic word meaning "neighbours") occupied the eastern territories of the right bank. The Germans intermarried with the few remaining Celts and with Illyrians from the Balkans and generally did little to support the fantasies of racial purity that became official doctrine between 1933 and 1945.

The Neanderthal Man was found in a quarry near Düsseldorf in 1856.

The Romans

From the beginning of recorded history, the Rhine served as a demarcation of power and conquest—in one direction or another. In 72 B.C. the Germanic king Ariovistus took 15,000 troops across the Rhine and conquered the part of Gaul that is now Alsace and the Palatinate (Rheinland-Pfalz). Gallic leaders called on the Romans for help and Julius Caesar defeated Ariovistus in 58 B.C., driving the Germans back across the Rhine. Three years later, Caesar himself crossed the Rhine, at Neuwied and declared the Gallic left bank a Roman protectorate.

The Romans halted their conquest of Germany at the Rhine when defeated by Arminius—or Hermann, as the Germans prefer to call him—in the battle of the Teutoburger Forest in A.D. 9. They retrenched on the Rhine's left bank, dividing it into Upper Germania, with headquarters at Mainz (Castrum Moguntiacum), and Lower Germania, with headquarters at Cologne.

Cologne had originally been established as the Oppidum Ubiorum, a town of resettlement for the Ubii, a friendly Germanic tribe brought across to the left bank in 38 B.C. by Augustus's general Agrippa. They built a port on the site of the present-day Heumarkt. A marble sculpture of Agrippa's head was found in excavations of the area and is now to be

Trier's Imperial Baths stood as a Roman bastion against the attacks of the unwashed barbarian hordes.

seen in Cologne's Römisch-Germanisches Museum (see pp. 36–37). Julia Agrippina, famed as the wife (and murderess) of Emperor Claudius, was born in the Oppidum Ubiorum; she later had it renamed Colonia Claudia Ara Agrippinensis—Colonia for short. You can see her head, too, in the museum, without a nose but with an elegant tightly curled hairdo.

In addition to Cologne, the Romans provided the Gallic

Rhineland with two other regional capitals, Trier* and Metz, and these subdivisions remained the basis for the Catholic Church's ecclesiastical districts right up to the French Revolution in 1789.

Frequent incursions from the turbulent Germanic tribes made the Roman Rhineland very much a beleaguered garrison, with eight legions in permanent encampment. To keep out the "barbarian" invaders, the Romans built a gigantic barrier, "Limes Germanicus", like Hadrian's Wall between England and Scotland. The dry moat and embankment, with a palisade and fortified towers every 10 miles, ran along the Romans' eastern frontier on the right bank of the Rhine from a point opposite Andernach up river as far as the Taunus ridge and then along the river Main. It worked for a while.

This permanent Roman presence was to give a markedly Latinized character to the civilization west of the Rhine. It also accounted for the region's sturdy resistance to the more Germanic tendencies of Martin Luther's Protestant Reformation and also, many historians

---

* Historically known as Treves in English.

feel, for the Rhineland's separatist aspirations in the 19th and even 20th centuries. The Romans certainly did leave a more "Mediterranean" tone in the Rhineland, especially with regard to festivities. It was, after all, the Romans who brought the grape.

The Barbarians

The decaying Roman imperial machine gradually buckled under pressure from barbarian invasions in the 4th century A.D. The Limes was breached, and the Germanic armies crossed over the frozen Rhine with their wagons—the climate was considerably colder than today. In 355 the Alemanni conquered in quick succession Worms, Speyer, Strasbourg, Mainz and Cologne. For the time being at least, only Trier resisted, under the leadership of future emperor Julian the Apostate.

The next wave of conquerors were the Burgundians, who set up court at Worms under Gundahar—the Gunther of the Nibelung legend. The Burgundians' capital was destroyed by the Huns in 436, at the instigation of the Roman commander Aëtius.

The Burgundians were driven west and turmoil in the Rhineland continued with wars

Nasty Nibelungs

The murky and confused legend of the Nibelungs comes to us from the Dark Ages. The Nibelungs were evil dwarfs, keepers of a huge treasure with a curse on it.

Siegfried, a brave prince from the north, won the treasure away from them and went on to Worms to woo Kriemhild, sister of King Gunther. Gunther had his eye on the fierce Icelandic queen, Brunhild, and Siegfried offered to go and get her. After great difficulties, he managed to bring Brunhild back to marry Gunther. But Brunhild, who felt she had been duped, had Gunther's henchman, Hagen, kill Siegfried.

Poor Kriemhild was left with only the Nibelung treasure and then Hagen took even that away and dumped it into the Rhine. Vowing revenge, Kriemhild married Attila, so that his Huns would punish Brunhild, Hagen and company. It all ended with a great blood bath, which inspired Richard Wagner to write four days' worth of operas.

between the Alemanni and the Franks. Under Clovis and his dynasty of Merovingian kings, the Franks achieved supremacy among the Germanic tribes with a growing policy of Christianization. By 742 Mainz had become the ecclesiastical capital of Germany with the nomination of Wynfrith (later St. Boniface) as archbishop.

At the beginning of the 9th century, Charlemagne established a Christian European empire and built his imperial palace at Aachen (Aix-la-Chapelle) on the western edge of the Rhineland. By cleverly manipulated propaganda—the popes wanted the empire to give their spiritual authority some military muscle—Charlemagne emerged with a quite virtuous image. According to one anonymous poet of his day: "Scholarly, modest, master of the world, beloved of the people... heroic, august and pious." But the facts of his life showed him spending most of the 47 years of his reign in warfare against those Germanic tribes that did not embrace the Christian faith. He massacred recalcitrants, imposed baptism on the meek and wholesale deportation of those who did not submit. He liked to gather scholars at his court, but Charlemagne himself gave little evidence of the intellectual qualities attributed to him. When he wasn't at war, he was out hunting. He never learned to write.

To some, Charlemagne was the first true Christian and European monarch; to others, just another barbarian. The views are not really contradictory, as the subsequent history of the Middle Ages was to show.

After Charlemagne's death, the empire was divided up among his grandsons. The eastern part eventually became the first German kingdom.

Crusading Zeal

Between 1096 and 1212 the Rhineland was a major centre for recruiting men, women—and children—for the Crusades to rescue Jerusalem from the Infidel. Peter the Hermit, an itinerant monk from Amiens, arrived in Cologne at Easter 1096 with thousands of Frenchmen eager to fight for the good cause. His fervent preaching aroused many more thousands of devout followers, but the Rhinelanders felt that, like charity, the massacre of "unbelievers" for the good of the Christian ideal should begin at home.

The handiest infidels were the Jews, who had settled in the Rhineland with the encouragement of the local archbishops, building Germany's first synagogue at Worms in 1034. The poorer Crusaders of the region were heavily in debt to the Jewish money-lenders—a profession forbidden to 17

Christians and one of the few open to Jews. About the easiest way to get rid of the debts was to get rid of the Jews. While the French pushed on to the Holy Land, the Rhinelanders went on a murderous rampage through the Jewish communities of Speyer, Worms, Mainz, Cologne and Trier, despite some archibishops' efforts to provide sanctuary. In the sunny little wine village of Rüdesheim, the rabbi and 50 of his congregation were offered conversion as a way out. They declined and were killed. The pattern of preliminary pogroms was repeated 50 years later, in 1146, at the urging of a fanatical Cistercian monk named Rudolf.

The period from the Crusades to the end of the Middle Ages saw the affirmation of the Holy Roman Empire—the

Rhenish Catholicism found serene expression in Lochner's Madonnas.

extension of Charlemagne's dream—and the archbishops of Mainz, Cologne and Trier were the most important of the emperor's electors. Their preeminence gave their cities and the Rhineland in general a political power and prestige which balanced any absolutist tendencies on the part of the emperor. His imperial diets (legislative sessions) were held at Speyer and Worms.

In 1184, Frederick Barbarossa chose Mainz as the site of a sumptuous celebration to honour his imperial glory, inviting 70,000 nobles from all over Europe for the feast of Pentecost. Mainz won the name of Aurea Moguntia (Golden Mainz) and was the only city besides Rome entitled to bear the ecclesiastical title of Holy Seat. These centuries were in general a golden age of prosperity for the Rhineland.

Luther Pays a Visit

In the mid-15th century, Johannes Gutenberg brought lasting glory to Mainz with his development of the printing press (see p. 66). But, paradoxically, his invention helped undermine the power of this seat of Catholic orthodoxy. Gutenberg's press gave greater currency not only to the Bible and the word of the Church but also to the ideas of those who disagreed with the Church, preparing the way for a popular movement to reform Catholicism and its German stronghold in the Rhineland.

Appropriately enough, the great confrontation between the Reformation leader Martin Luther and the Vatican's representatives in Germany took place in the Rhineland. That was at the Imperial Diet of Worms in April 1521, three months after Luther's excommunication for opposing official doctrine. The papal nuncio had done everything possible to keep Luther away from Worms, rightly foreseeing an enormous propaganda success for the Reformation cause if he came. An emissary rode out to tell Luther he would be killed by his enemies if he dared to enter Worms, and Luther replied: "Tell your master that if there were as many devils at Worms as tiles on its roofs, I would enter." Safely inside Worms, where he encountered more supporters than devils, Luther refused to recant, "for it is neither safe nor right to act against one's conscience. God help me. Amen."*

---

* It remains a matter of debate among historians whether Luther actually said the famous: "Here I stand, I can do no other."

The Catholic Rhineland withstood the doctrinal onslaught of the Reformation only after decades of strife and open warfare. In 1541, archbishop of Cologne Hermann von Wied, who tried to make some compromises with the new ideas, was promptly excommunicated. Four years later the Jesuits settled in Cologne and attempted to bring the dissidents into line. The situation was complicated by the fact that local rulers appreciated the political implications of Luther's tenets—defiance of Rome, but obedience to one's secular lord.

More trouble came with the choice of Gebhard Truchsess von Waldburg as archbishop and elector of Cologne. This good Jesuit went astray when he fell passionately in love with Countess Agnes von Mansfeld, canoness of the Gerresheim convent near Düsseldorf. He began to find the new tenets of Protestantism increasingly attractive. With the military support of Rhineland nobles such as Johann von Nassau, he announced his Protestant allegiance on Christmas 1582 and the next year celebrated a riotous wedding with the canoness. Under the Jesuit leadership of Petrus Canisius, the Catholic Church brought in

Bavarian troops to crush the rebels. After a devastating war, Gebhard was exiled and Duke Ernst of Bavaria, bishop of Freising, came reluctantly to replace him in Cologne. The Jesuits were obliged to let the bishop bring along his many lady-friends, but at least they had a doctrinally orthodox prelate again.

The Rhineland remained a bastion of Catholicism but continued as a battlefield for the wars with the Protestants.

Martin Luther's 1521 visit to Worms is commemorated with this group of statues of Protestant heroes in the heart of Catholic Rhineland.

Scorched Earth

During the Thirty Years' War (1618–48), in which dynastic, religious and international power struggles were intertwined, Gustavus Adolphus of Sweden introduced the Asiatic military concept of "scorched earth" to Europe, plundering, burning and laying total waste to the invaded territory so that his enemies had nothing left to live on after his army departed. It was the Rhinelanders' misfortune to live in an area subjected to this policy.

In the struggles between Catholics and Protestants, Habsburgs and Bourbons, the Rhinelanders watched helplessly as the armies passed back and forth across their lands. **21**

There was no way of telling friend from enemy. Civilians were plundered, raped and massacred by all sides as German, Spanish and French troops quickly adopted the Swedish tactics. In the churches along the Rhine, Protestant soldiers gouged out the eyes of statues of the Virgin Mary. In the village of Bacharach, eight times besieged and captured by one side or another, the people were reduced to eating grass. Mainz—which had the doubtful honour of providing Gustavus Adolphus with his winter quarters in 1631—was left in such ruins that visiting travellers were obliged to sleep in boats on the river. Cologne, by observing a scrupulous neutrality behind its fortified walls, was one of the few Rhenish towns to escape destruction. By the end of the war, the princes had to encourage their surviving subjects to resort to polygamy in order to repopulate the desolated region.

Having pursued a clever policy of playing off one side against the other, Cardinal Richelieu and his protégé and successor Mazarin were able to win Alsace for France at the Treaty of Westphalia which ended the war. In doing so, they established a French foothold on the Rhine and set the stage for future Franco-German conflict over the coveted Rhineland territories.

Cardinal Mazarin promoted the formation of a Rhine league, uniting the Rhenish princes and bishops of the Palatinate and Hesse under the leadership of the archbishop of Mainz. Created to defend "the German liberties" and act as a buffer between the French and the Habsburgs, the league lasted only ten years, till 1668, when Louis XIV decided that the Rhine and the Palatinate were desirable territories. But he failed to get his French candidate nominated as archbishop of Cologne and was equally unsuccessful claiming the Palatinate for his brother's wife Liselotte after the death of her father, the Elector Palatinate. In 1689, he sent the French armies on an expedition that made the Swedes look good by comparison. Under the brutal command of François Louvois, they burned over 100 towns in the Rhineland and Palatinate, including Boppard, Bingen, Oppenheim, Worms, Speyer, Mannheim and Heidelberg.

The French Revolution

The 18th century ushered in a period of relative peace, reconstruction and, most important, repopulation. The Rhenish princes enjoyed their rococo fun and games, imitating the frills and frolics of Versailles. In the students' debates at the University of Mainz could be heard the first echos of another new French fashion—the Revolution. The new talk of liberty and equality appealed greatly to the young radicals but less so to the princes, especially when they heard the French Revolutionaries pick up the old refrain about France's "natural frontiers, the Alps and the Rhine"—going back to Julius Caesar for justification. Sure enough, in the autumn of 1792, French Revolutionary troops under the Comte de Custine arrived to "liberate" Speyer, Worms, Mainz and Frankfurt. Cajoled by Custine, Mainz proceeded to vote for annexation to France. General Lazare Hoche took over command and encouraged the German nationalist Joseph Görres to work for a Rhenish republic, but the idea died with Hoche in 1797. Instead the left bank of the Rhine was carved up into four French *départements*. The old Gallic dream seemed fulfilled.

In 1806 Napoleon created the Confederation of the Rhine as part of his dismantling of that old Holy Roman Empire which, as historians agreed, was only briefly a real empire, never Roman and scarcely ever holy. The archbishops of Mainz, Cologne and Trier lost the last shred of their hereditary political power. The new arrangement gave the Rhinelanders the privileges of providing 63,000 soldiers for Napoleon and paying for the upkeep of the French soldiers garrisoned on their territory. But the Rhenish bourgeoisie didn't complain too loudly because Napoleon did boost the economy with factories springing up between Cologne and Aachen, new land developed for agriculture and modern roads along the Rhine for swift troop movement. He also emancipated the Jews, enabling the Rothschilds and Oppenheimers to become members of the Electoral College in Frankfurt.

Enter the Prussians

In 1813 Napoleon was driven back across the Rhine into France, hotly pursued by Prussian General Blücher, whose crossing of the ice-covered river is commemorated to this day by his statue at Kaub. After Napoleon's defeat, the 1815 Congress of Vienna handed the Rhineland over to Prussia, **23** an idea of Britain's Lord Castlereagh, to provide a counterweight to Austria and France. Acquiescing in this reapportionment of the Rhineland was one of its most illustrious sons, scion of an old Koblenz family, Austrian Chancellor Metternich—the Congress's mastermind.

Prussian aristocratic conservatism constantly clashed with the Rhineland's liberal-minded bourgeoisie. The Prussians suppressed Joseph Görres's outspoken newspaper, the *Rheinischer Merkur,* but progressive Rhenish capitalists subsequently turned to a young fellow from Trier named Karl Marx to edit their *Rheinische Zeitung* in opposition to the conservative-clerical *Kölner Zeitung.* At the age of 24, Marx was happy to provide his employers with scrupulously orthodox liberal economic articles, devoting the rest of the paper to vehemently radical attacks on exploitative landowners and reactionary Russia, Prussia's chief ally. It was a protest by Czar Nicholas I himself that finally prompted the Prussians to close down the paper. Marx's editorship lasted six months, during which time he learned the art of polemic— and of making a profit for the owners.

The Rhineland remained a hotbed of unrest, and the 1848 revolts spread from France like a brushfire through Heidelberg, Mannheim, Mainz and Cologne. In Cologne, radicals sang "La Marseillaise", but the new liberal ideals were mixed with a strong dose of German nationalism that was ready to resist renewed French claims on the Rhineland. For the

Karl Marx learned a lot about polemics writing for a Cologne paper.

French had begun talking again about their "natural frontiers" and the Germans sang in response "Die Wacht am Rhein" (Watch on the Rhine), urging the people: "To the Rhine, to the Rhine, to the German Rhine! Along the river, who'll mount the guard?"

The answer, of course, was the Prussians, and Chancellor Otto von Bismarck quickly squashed any lingering Rhenish thoughts of separatism.

War with France

Conflict with the French came to a head in 1870 while King Wilhelm of Prussia was taking the waters at the spa town of Bad Ems, 10 miles across the river from Koblenz. His confrontation there with the French ambassador over rival French and Prussian efforts to influence succession to the Spanish throne was manipulated by Bismarck in a provocative telegram leaked to the press to incite France to declare war. German victory forced the French back from the Rhine, taking away Alsace and Lorraine. And the king of Prussia was proclaimed emperor of the new Germany.

More than ever the Rhine became a festering symbol of Franco-German hostility. When revenge came with the Allied victory over Germany in World War I, the French, besides retrieving Alsace and Lorraine, revived their old obsession with the territory on the Rhine's left bank. At the Versailles peace conference, pushing for an independent Rhenish Republic under French supervision, Marshal Ferdinand Foch said: "The Rhine alone is important. Nothing else matters." French occupying troops encouraged Rhenish separatists—among them the mayor of Cologne Konrad Adenauer—to stage a coup d'état on June 1, 1919. An obscure bureaucrat, Dr. Hans Adam Dorten, was declared president of the new republic, with its capital at Wiesbaden. It lasted only a few hours, until Prime Minister Georges Clemenceau, under Anglo-American pressure, sent orders to break it up.

French military occupation of the Rhineland continued, though with passive German resistance in the form of strikes and sabotage, until final evacuation in 1930 in keeping with the Locarno agreement under which the Rhineland was to remain demilitarized.

The Third Reich

Then came Hitler. He moved troops into the Rhineland in

1936 and celebrated the event with a triumphant speech from Cologne cathedral and was showered with flowers as he paraded through Trier and Aachen. Amazed at the lack of French reaction, Hitler said later: "I had only four brigades. If we had been obliged to retreat, the Reich would have collapsed."

As the rest of Europe remained uncertain and divided, the Nazi appetite for conquest proved to be insatiable. The consequences were seen belatedly in September 1938, when Britain's Neville Chamberlain came to Bad Godesberg during the "Munich Crisis" to discuss Czechoslovakia with Hitler. As Chamberlain drove down to the ferry that was to take him across to the Petersberg Hotel high above the Rhine, swastikas flew side by side with Union Jacks in the sleepy little spa town that is now Bonn's diplomatic suburb. Hitler came by yacht and stayed at the riverside Dreesen Hotel where he raged and stormed at Chamberlain for three hours over Germany's right to occupy the Sudetenland, the predominantly German-speaking part of Czechoslovakia. After a second more conciliatory late-night talk, Chamberlain told Hitler: "I have the feeling a relationship of confidence has grown up between us."

There followed the notorious meeting in Munich and the German annexation of the Sudetenland. And by Novem-

Bonn is becoming a modern capital almost entirely against its will.

ber, the Rhineland, as elsewhere in Germany, was lit up by the flames of synagogues burning in the centuries-old Jewish communities of Cologne, Koblenz, Mainz and Worms, on the infamous Kristallnacht (Crystal Night) that was to launch the Holocaust.

In the war that ensued, the Rhineland was the first region to suffer the retaliatory mass bombing attacks on civilian targets. On the night of May 30, 1942, Britain's bombers devastated Cologne. Countless thousands died and thousands more fled as the city's population shrank from 800,000 in 1939 to 40,000 in 1945. Along

the Rhine, Mainz, Koblenz, Bonn and Düsseldorf all suffered similar losses. In February 1945, the Allied forces with 85 divisions occupied the left bank. The retreating Germans blew up all the Rhine bridges except the Ludendorff railway bridge at Remagen and, on March 7, the United States 9th Armored Division of the 1st Army arrived to establish a bridgehead for the drive east. Patton's 3rd Army crossed at Oppenheim. The Rhineland they moved through had been levelled not only by Allied bombing but also by zealous Germans who followed Hitler's order that "the battle should be conducted without consideration for our own population—destroy everything, including food and clothing stores."

Post-War Miracle

With the aid of the American Marshall Plan and their own muscle and energy, the Rhinelanders' reconstruction was spectacular. Konrad Adenauer, who became the first peacetime chancellor in 1949, stubbornly championed the cause of Bonn in his beloved Rhineland as the new capital, against the claims of towns like Hamburg and Frankfurt. Originally considered merely "provi-

Finding Your Way...
Here are some common terms you may come across in the Rhine Valley:

Allee	boulevard
Bahnhof	railway station
Brücke	bridge
Brunnen	fountain
Burg	castle, fortress
Dom	cathedral
Gasse	alley
Kirche	church
Markt	market
Rathaus	town hall
Platz	square
Schloß*	castle, palace
Stift	monastery
Straße	street
Ufer	river bank
Weg	path, way

sional" pending the reunification of East and West Germany, Bonn has gradually settled into its governmental role. Long-time residents complain of the oppressive nature of Bonn's often heavy, muggy climate, but now it's no longer clear whether the cause of the headaches is meteorological or political.

Despite occasional scares of political terrorism—armoured personnel carriers regularly patrol government buildings and diplomatic residences—the Rhineland enjoys today a life of ease and prosperity.

28

* read ß as ss.

Where to Go

The Rhine is a river and so should of course be seen by boat, but it's also the heart of a wide strip of interesting country that can be explored by car, train or bus. Try to cover it both by land and by water.

Although the Rhine flows from south to north, we recommend that you start the land part of your journey at Cologne, work your way south and then take a boat back, going downstream. It is fascinating to see how different the same place looks from the river and from the shore, and even more different are views of the castles, vineyards and rocky landscapes of the heart of the Rhine Valley when approached from the south or the north.

It's a good idea to plan your itinerary carefully so you can just sit back and enjoy romantic dreams.

Riverboat Shuffle

It was the British who first took a steamboat up the Rhine in 1816 from the North Sea to Cologne. The Germans liked the idea and soon had a company going with a name almost as long as the river—the Preussisch-Rheinische Dampfschiffahrts-Gesellschaft Köln. It was the precursor of today's Köln-Düsseldorfer, known in these more hurried times as the KD. The modern fleet is almost entirely motor-powered with only few steam-driven paddleboats for nostalgia.

The trip through the heart of the Rhine Valley enables you—with a certain effort of imagination—to see the river as sailors of the Middle Ages saw it. In the shadow of the towering cliffs they navigated uncertainly through the rocks at the mercy of pirates, robber-barons and any petty prince who cared to claim a toll from them at the point of a sword. About the only risk you run today as you pass the treacherous Lorelei (see p. 57) is not being able to keep up with the words of the song as they come over the ship's loudspeakers. If your German is rusty, console yourself with the song's first line: *"Ich weiss nicht, was soll es bedeuten…"* (I don't know what it means…).

If you are travelling by train or bus and want to cover the whole territory described here, you can start out in Cologne and go down to Koblenz via Bonn. Then strike out along the river Mosel for the first of the excursions, as far as Trier. Take a trip into the Eifel countryside on your way back to Koblenz or drive through the Hunsrück. Pick up the Rhine again at Koblenz and continue through the valley to Wiesbaden and Mainz. Here you can go out on the next excursion south to Heidelberg and back via Speyer and Worms. From there head for the Taunus hills before embarking on a river-boat trip from any of the wine-village stops of Eltville, Oestrich or Rüdesheim at least as far as Koblenz. The river trip is less interesting north of here and you might prefer to return on the train or bus and go on a last excursion to Düsseldorf.

If you have a car and want to include a boat trip, you can modify this itinerary a little by leaving your car at, say, Koblenz, going south by train and then returning by boat to pick up your car for inland excursions. It's really worthwhile working out the little logistics in advance to get the maximum diversity out of your trip.

Cologne *(Köln)*
Pop. 980,000

For a first taste of the Rhineland's mixture of the practical and the romantic, the serious and the humorous, there's nowhere better to begin than Cologne. And in Cologne the starting point is inevitably the **cathedral** *(Dom).*

After the devastating bombardments of World War II, it was literally one of the few buildings left standing, defiantly dominating the city.

Today, amid Cologne's shining rebuilt prosperity, elevated on a terrace like a somewhat haughty dignitary, the cathedral, now dedicated to St. Peter and Mary, occupies a position that has been sacred since Roman times. Around A. D. 50, it was the site of the Temple of Mercurius Augustus. The first Christian church was built there in the 4th century by Bishop Maternus.

Progressively expanded over the next few centuries, the church began to burst at its seams in the 13th century when thousands of pilgrims flocked to Cologne to view the shrine containing the relics of the Three Kings. In 1248 the church was replaced with a cathedral conceived on a gigantic Gothic plan, inspired by the French cathedrals of Amiens and Rheims. Work went on for 300 years and then halted for lack of funds, with the steeples still unbuilt. The church remained that way for another 300 years until, at the urging of the young German Romantics and nationalists, work was resumed and the steeples completed in 1880.

Those steeples are naturally the first thing you see of the cathedral, the first thing you see of Cologne, in fact. But, imposing and even grandiose as they are, their effect is a little frigid, too symmetrical for those who would have liked the 19th-century architects to have followed rather less faithfully the 600-year-old plans that were miraculously rediscovered in Darmstadt and in Paris. As it is, they complete the largest façade—200 feet wide, 515 feet high—of any church in Christendom.

Inside, the true architectural glory of the cathedral is its **choir,** a magnificent example of 13th-century Gothic intensity, its slim, almost delicate lines contrasting strikingly with the massiveness of the whole edifice. Very impressive in their natural elegance, set on the pillars of the choir, are the statues of Christ and Mary flanked by the apostles, sculpted by Master Arnold, one of the building's original architects. Take a good look, too, at the richly carved oak choir-stalls, with their mythical animals, musi-

Cologne's majestic cathedral is the dominant point of the pious old traditions of the Rhineland.

cians, dancers, lovers and warriors.

The cathedral's richest treasure, looking itself like a basilica, is the gold **Dreikönigenschrein** (Shrine of the Three Kings) behind the High Altar. The bones of the Three Kings were brought by Friedrich Barbarossa's chancellor, Reinald von Dassel, from Milan in the 12th century. Nikolaus von Verdun was commissioned to design this masterpiece of the goldsmith's art. Begun in 1181, it took 40 years to complete. The solid gold figures include the kings and prophets of the Old Testament along with scenes of Christ's baptism and

the adoration of the Kings. Each of the Three Kings' skeletons lacks a finger, donated to Hildesheim (near Hanover) where Dassel had been dean.

Another highly prized work is Stephan Lochner's splendid 15th-century **Dombild,** a triptych to the right of the choir celebrating the patron saints of Cologne—Ursula, Gereon and the Three Kings. Ursula is said to have been an English girl who in the 4th century led a pilgrimage of 11,000 virgins to Rome, all of whom were massacred by the Huns at Cologne on their way home. On the left side of the choir is the fine 10th-century **Gerokreuz** (Gero

The Shrine of the Three Kings is a triumph of the goldsmith's art.

Cross), named after Archbishop Gero who commissioned this movingly simple crucifixion. It is the earliest example of a Byzantine-style sculpture appearing in Western Europe. In the Sakramentskapelle is the beautiful **Milan Madonna,** sculpted around 1280, with the colour, crown and sceptre restored last century.

Appropriately enough, next door to this formidable Christian monument, in the **Römisch-Germanisches Museum,** is the delightfully pagan Roman tribute to Bacchanalian pleasure, the **Dionysos Mosaic.** One of the few nice things to have happened in Cologne during World War II was the discovery of this marvellously well-preserved work in the course of digging an air-raid shelter. The museum in which it is now housed was built around the mosaic's original site, once the floor of a prosperous 3rd-century Roman wheat merchant's dining-room. Dionysos is the Greek name of the fun-loving god the Romans called Bacchus. You can see him leaning tipsily on an obliging satyr while around him other satyrs and nymphs cavort and make music. This, too, is Cologne.

The museum itself is a wonderfully unstuffy way to discover the city's Roman origins. Light and airy, it is designed not as a museum of ancient works of art so much as a showplace for the everyday life of the Romans of Colonia and their Germanic neighbours. With excellent multilingual audio-visual aids, you'll see the artefacts of the early settlers' homes and workshops, their religion and political administration.

The postwar reconstruction of Cologne has generally been a boon for the reorganization of its museums and particularly the Rhineland's most important art gallery, the **Wallraf-Richartz-Museum.** Situated on the Wallrafplatz a short walk south-west of the cathedral, the pleasant modern building is a triumph of imaginative lighting and display for an excellent collection of early Rhenish art and many fine examples of the great European painters. Based originally on the private collection of Ferdinand Wallraf (1748–1824), its most significant offering is the work of the flourishing Cologne School of the 14th to 16th centuries, culminating in the masterpieces of Stephan Lochner. The best of his paintings here are the monumental **Day of Judgement** and the delicate **Virgin and Child in the Rose Bower,** each showing the sensitive use of colour and serenity of form that characterized the Cologne School. For a view of Cologne in the 15th century, look at the anonymous 1411 painting of St. Ursula, with just a few of her 11,000 virgins sailing past the town as it appeared a thousand years after her death.

Other great German art in the museum includes Albrecht Dürer's *Piper and Drummer*, a lighter side of the early Renaissance master, Lucas Cranach's beautifully ornate *Saint Mary* **37**

Magdalene, and Hans Burgkmair's mysteriously challenging *Portrait of the Schellenbergers.*

The Flemish and Dutch are well represented, and the French do very nicely with Claude Lorrain, François Boucher and Gustave Courbet, as well as a good collection of Impressionists.

Above the Wallraf-Richartz in the same building is the **Museum Ludwig,** devoted to modern art—Picasso, Dali, Klee, Kandinsky and Max Ernst—but it is perhaps most remarkable for the comprehensive American Pop Art collection. There is something especially pleasing about a building that houses both the exquisite, anonymous 15th-century Gothic *Madonna with Pea Blossom* and Claes Oldenburg's lusty *Giant Soft Swedish Light Switch.*

One other museum worth your attention is the **Schnütgen** on the Cäcilienstrasse. In terms of political prestige and commercial prosperity, the Middle Ages were undoubtedly Cologne's heyday and the Schnütgen offers a superb collection of the best Romanesque and Gothic art work produced in and around Cologne. In the converted St. Cecilia church, work in ivory, gold and wood is very artfully displayed. Noteworthy are the painted wood *Christ on a Donkey* and among many fine madonnas—the 12th-century *Siegburger* and the 13th-century *Aachener Madonna.*

In a region whose architectural past has been progressively obliterated by successive wars and revolutions, the Schnütgen's sculpture collection admirably preserves these vestiges of the Rhineland's golden past. For just a hint of what the old town of Cologne used to look like, go back to the river, to the tiny **Altstadt** between the Gross St. Martin church and the Deutzer bridge. There, around the old Fischmarkt, along the Salzgasse and across the Eisenmarkt (Ironware Market), you can find miracles of survival and restoration of houses dating back to the 13th and 14th centuries. Now a thriving, renewed neighbourhood of restaurants, antique shops, art galleries and apartments with attractive gardens, the lively atmosphere helps you imagine what it was like in the good old days.

But Cologne also has a bouncing, bustling present attested by the gleaming, pedestrians-only commercial area along the Hohe Strasse southwest of the cathedral. Re-

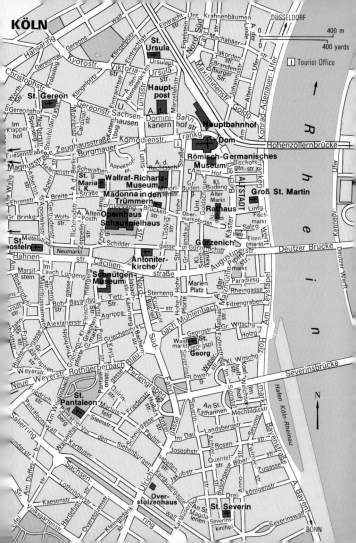

KÖLN

DÜSSELDORF

400 m

400 yards

i Tourist Office

St. Ursula

St. Gereon

Hauptpost

Hauptbahnhof

Dom

Römisch-Germanisches Museum

St. Maria

Wallraf-Richartz-Museum

Madonna in den Trümmern

Opernhaus

Schauspielhaus

Groß St. Martin

Rathaus

Gürzenich

St. Aposteln

Antoniter-kirche

Schnütgen-Museum

St. Georg

St. Pantaleon

Hohenzollernbrücke

Deutzer Brücke

Severinsbrücke

ALTSTADT

Hafen Köln-Rheinau

R h e i n

N

Overstolzenhaus

St. Severin

BONN

flecting its taste for things French, the town offers plenty of outdoor cafés. Some of the most agreeable are around Am Hof where you can linger over a delicious pastry and coffee while contemplating the delightfully kitschy dwarfs and inquisitive tailoress of the Heinzelmännchenbrunnen (Heinzeldwarf's Well) sculpted in 1899.

To round off the church scene, you might like to look in the **Antoniterkirche** (on the Schildergasse), the main church of the small Protestant community, and admire Ernst Barlach's 1927 sculpture *Der Trauernde Engel* (the Mourning Angel)—to which he has given the features of his fellow artist Käthe Kollwitz. The best of the city's Romanesque churches, indeed one of the most delicate in the Rhineland, is the **St. Aposteln** west of the Neumarkt on the Mittelstrasse. The apse is decorated with blind arcades and graceful galleries. But perhaps the most moving of Cologne's many ecclesiastical edifices is the **Madonna in den Trümmern** (Madonna in the Ruins), the modern chapel built out of the rubble of the old Gothic St. Kolumba church on Brücken-strasse. World War II bombardments left standing only the stump of a tower and part of one outer wall. Amazingly, a statue of the Virgin Mary also emerged unscathed. Hence the name of the chapel, which Gottfried Böhm designed in the 1950s, artfully integrating modern simplicity with the Gothic remains. Here you'll get a true feeling of the city's history of pain and recovery.

On the western side of the Alter Markt (where you might notice in passing the statue of the *Kallendresser* baring his

bottom to no one in particular—very typical Cologne humour) is the proud old **Rathaus** or Town Hall. Its elegant Renaissance pillared loggia is as warm and inviting as the administrative extension of its modern Spanischer Bau is cold and forbidding. From the Rathaus, the Judengasse, once the main street of the medieval Jewish quarter, takes you to the **Gürzenich,** home of historic merriment. Cologne's most important secular Gothic building —and practically the only one to survive into this century—was designed as a dance hall for the city government and its honoured guests, including the occasional Habsburg or Hohenzollern. It is still the most prestigious venue for Carnival balls, banquets and concerts, the perfect Gothic complement to the cathedral.

Trace Cologne's beginnings in the Römisch-Germanisches Museum.

South to Koblenz

On the way to Bonn, you can make a pleasant side-trip to BRÜHL to visit the Augustusburg castle. This delightful baroque residence, with its sculptured, landscaped gardens and charming Falkenlust hunting pavilion, takes you back to a fairytale world where its 18th-century owner, the elector and archbishop of Cologne Clemens August, liked to indulge his extra-ecclesiastical in- terests. **Schloss Brühl,** as it's commonly known, bears wit- ness to the Rhenish princes' infatuation with French style and the aura of Versailles. The château and hunting pavilion were designed by François de Cuvilliés, Belgian by birth, Bavarian by choice; but to en- sure authenticity the gardens were entrusted to a French- man, Dominique Girard. By all means, stroll around the in- tricate geometry of the gardens and imagine the rustle of crino-

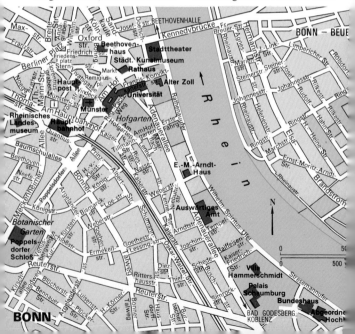

lines, but don't fail to go inside the Augustusburg to see the opulent staircase. As you will find, there's nothing austere about being a Catholic in the Rhineland.

Bonn

Pop. 283,000

Not many people take Bonn seriously as the capital of West Germany—least of all the Germans themselves. This is as much a tribute to its quiet serenity as a complaint about its lack of dynamism. But Bonn does have a modest charm, rather a nice surprise for the seat of government of such a busy, purposeful, self-confident nation.

To get a feeling for the atmosphere in which the country conducts its official business, start at the complex of government buildings between the Rhine and the very properly named Adenauerallee. The **Bundeshaus,** the parliament, offers multilingual guided tours when not in session. There's a fine view of the Siebengebirge (Seven Hills) across the river from the public restaurant on the 30th floor of the Abgeordnetenhochhaus (Deputies' Building); open Friday evenings, Sundays and days when parliament is not convened. Nearby are the Palais Schaum-

burg, the chancellor's former residence now used for entertaining international guests, and the Villa Hammerschmidt, official home of the federal president, both 19th-century versions of the Renaissance style.

All very efficient and businesslike, but now change gears with a restful stroll at the other end of the Adenauerallee, around the old trees of the **Hofgarten.** This leads back to the university, housed in the elegant baroque residence designed for the high-living elector of Cologne Joseph Clemens by Louis XIV's architect Robert de Cotte. It was in the elector's private chapel here that a bright 16-year-old Bonn schoolboy named Ludwig van Beethoven performed his first music. The residence was linked by a long avenue to the Poppelsdorfer Schloss in the university's botanical gardens; the remains of the castle have been restored after heavy war damage.

Bonn's sunny baroque style can be appreciated in the graceful **Rathaus** (Town Hall) with its balustraded outside staircase, very much the centre of the "quiet" city basking in its 18th-century dream. The shopping area, like Cologne's blocked off from traffic, keeps **43** things in the subdued mode. The affairs of state seem a long way away.

Beethoven was born in Bonn in 1770 and his birthplace, the **Beethovenhaus,** at Bonngasse 20, has been preserved as a museum, proudly claiming the largest and most valuable collection of Beethoven memorabilia. It includes one of the grand pianos he played towards the end of his life and the acoustical instruments he used to combat his increasing deafness. Beethoven went to Vienna at the age of 22 to escape from his alcoholic father, but Bonn itself had not been too unkind to him. He gained

an introduction to the high society of the elector's court where his father sang as tenor in the chapel. And he found particular favour with the von Breuning family, falling hopelessly in love with one of the daughters, Eleonore.

The best of Bonn's museums is the **Rheinisches Landes-**

museum, outstanding for its Rhenish painters with some fine examples of the Cologne School. But the stars are undoubtedly the **Neanderthal Man** and **Cro-Magnon Couple.** Old Neanderthal, 50,000 years old in fact, was found by workmen in a quarry near Düsseldorf in 1856. His remains include the top of his skull and 16 other bones, enough for anthropologists to determine that he was 5 feet 4 inches tall and 60 years old when he died. He hunted animals like the mammoth, whose remains you can also see on the wall nearby. The Cro-Magnon man and woman, dating back to 10,000 B.C., are displayed with carved bone figures buried with them in their grave. Anthropologists deduce that these were symbolic of the animals they were accustomed to eat and were placed beside their corpses to provide them with ritual food for the afterlife.

You should also stop off at the municipal art museum, **Städtisches Kunstmuseum** (next to the Rathaus) to see the important collection of the work of August Macke, a lead-

A Bonn University student can sit in the Hofgarten and forget that the German government even exists. **45**

ing member of the Blaue Reiter school of German Expressionists. The 12th-century Romanesque church, the Münster, has been harmed more by insensitive restoration in the 19th century than by the destruction of World War II, but the **cloister** on the south side is for many people the prettiest, most peaceful spot in Bonn.

Bad Godesberg, which enjoyed its heyday in the 19th century as a smart spa resort, has retained an old-fashioned elegance for its new role as Bonn's diplomatic suburb. The ambassadors' Biedermeier residences are guarded from the threat of latter-day political terrorism by regular patrols of armoured vehicles. Their incongruous passage through the tree-shaded streets has been accepted as part of the natural landscape of a beleaguered capital.

Godesberg entered history as host to the fateful 1938 meeting between Hitler and Chamberlain (see p. 26). Now a slightly wistful memory of past "glory", the Dreesen, always a favourite haunt of the Führer, offers a good view from its terrace of the Siebengebirge (most notably the Drachenfels, Ölberg and Petersberg), with the old Hotel Petersberg perched high up on the other side of the river. There Chamberlain, Haile Selassie, Queen Elizabeth and Leonid Brezhnev have stayed. The hotel is now being converted to a state guesthouse.

If you take the Autobahn 61 south to Koblenz, interrupt the journey at the **Laacher See,** west of ANDERNACH, for a look at the fascinating volcanic crater lake. A typical formation of the huge Eifel plateau, the lake, 5 miles in circumference, is surrounded by the cones of extinct volcanoes. Perhaps the most attractive spot to observe from is the fine 11th- and 12th-century Benedictine abbey of **Maria Laach** at the south-west tip. The graceful six-towered church stands squarely in the Rhenish Romanesque tradition of Mainz, Worms and Speyer, but offers a slightly gentler version of the ecclesiastical fortress because of the delightful colonnaded cloister-garden, Paradies, by its western wall.

Koblenz

The town of Koblenz takes its name from the Latin *confluentes*, referring to the confluence of the Mosel and Rhine rivers. Its strategic position has been important throughout history. Economically, besides serving as a centre for the wines of the

Mosel and the Rhine, Koblenz levied tolls on the merchant-boats that passed from one river to the other. Politically, in the days before Napoleon, the elector and archbishop of Trier preferred Koblenz as a residence because he could keep an eye on both the Rhine and the Mosel. Today it provides the same convenience to tourists. Though over 80 per cent of it was destroyed in World War II, the town still offers an attractive glimpse of its past, plus a foretaste of the pleasures of wine sampling off to the west and south.

The most agreeable introduction to Koblenz is the walk along the **Rheinanlagen,** the airy river-promenade lined with maples and willows. The brainchild of a French prefect during the Napoleonic occupation of the Rhineland, the riverside park was laid out in its present form by Augusta, wife of Kaiser Wilhelm.

From the south the walk will take you past the Weindorf (wine village), a relic of the wine-fair held in 1925. Wine-tasting and dances are still held here. Continue past the **Kurfürstliches Schloss** (Elector's Palace), a fine example of 18th-century Rhenish-French neoclassical architecture. It's best viewed from the outside, admirably restored after the war, as the bombardment left little of the original interior intact.

Beyond the Schloss you'll follow the Rhine quay to **St. Kastor,** the town's most important church, a well-proportioned Romanesque edifice notable for the monumental Gothic tombs of two Trier archbishops, Kuno von Falkenstein and Werner von Königstein. North of the church, open-air operas and concerts are performed in the summertime in the striking setting of the Blumenhof, courtyard of the old Deutschherrenhaus (House of the Knights of the Teutonic Order). The Rhine promenade ends with the formidable **Deutsches Eck,** a gigantic monument erected for Kaiser Wilhelm I in 1897 and now dedicated to German unity. Displaying a huge eagle disposing of six serpents and two human enemies, the 72-foot monument is now just a pedestal—the kaiser's statue was knocked off in 1945—with the motto: "Never will the Reich be destroyed if you are unified and loyal." You can ponder this as you climb the 107 steps of the pedestal for a good view of the old town along the Mosel and the more modern construction along the Rhine.

Start your visit of the **Altstadt** (Old Town) at the splendid old **Balduinbrücke,** the 1343 bridge built across the Mosel by the powerful elector-archbishop Balduin, brother or Holy Roman Emperor Heinrich VII. The bridge withstood all the onslaughts of its long troubled history until a 1945 bomb destroyed 3 of the 14 arches and a new section had to be built linking a river island to the Mosel's north shore.

Coming back off the bridge you'll pass the castle-lodge, all that survives of the **Alte Burg** (Old Castle) destroyed by Louis XIV's troops in 1689, and now the municipal library. On the Münzplatz is the **Metternich-Hof,** birthplace of the wily chancellor of Austria Prince Klemens von Metternich. That Metternich ended up in the service of the Austrian government is less surprising than it seems. In the absence of a unified German nation, it was more natural for this old Catholic Rhineland family to turn to Vienna for a diplomatic career than to Protestant Prussian Berlin. Napoleon transformed Metternich's house into a law school, with instructions to its professors and students to work on the application of the Napoleonic Code to the Rhineland.

Today the Münzplatz has a lively flower, fruit and vegetable market. Take a look at the **Liebfrauenkirche,** whose handsome interior includes some remarkable Renaissance tombstones, and then explore the miraculously preserved vestiges of old Koblenz houses: the 14th-century Haus Kastorstrasse 2, and the charming **Vier Türme** on the corner of Am Plan and Löhrstrasse, a late 17th-century building with four oriels (or projecting bays), which you can find again in the early 18th-century guildhouses of the grocers *(Krämer)* on Kornpfortstrasse and of the shoemakers *(Schuhmacher)* on Görgenstrasse. These houses would have no special impact in a well-preserved old town, but in war-battered Koblenz, they stand out like precious jewels.

As a kind of aperitif to the castles you'll be seeing further south, end your visit to Koblenz with a trip across the Rhine to the fortress of **Ehrenbreitstein.** By car you go by way of the Pfaffendorfer Bridge with a steep but pleasant drive up to the ramparts.

48

Why not call some friends to join you for a drink at the Weinstube?

Pedestrians can take the ferry at the end of the Rheinstrasse and a chair-lift to the fortress. The foundations date back to the year 1000 when a knight named Heribert built himself a stronghold. It was taken over for the Holy Roman Empire by the archbishopric of Trier. The French blew it up in 1801, the Prussians rebuilt it, but the Versailles treaty of 1918 specified that the fortress not be used for military purposes. Today it's a youth hostel, restaurant and museum of prehistoric artefacts. Best of all, it's the perfect spot for a panoramic view of the Mosel and Rhine valleys. The castle you see to the south on the left bank is the Stolzenfels—neo-Gothic, a little bit Spanish, a little bit English, the way they built castles in 1825.

Koblenz's Balduin Bridge beckons you to the Mosel. But don't miss the charms of St. Severus, Boppard.

Rhine Valley

Geographically, of course, the whole length of the Rhine, from Switzerland to the North Sea, constitutes its "valley", but the Rhine Valley that people dream about is the part between Koblenz and Mainz. This is where the mountains of the Hunsrück on the west and the Taunus and Rheingau-Gebirge on the east come right down to the river forming a narrow valley of steeply terraced vineyards and pine forests guarded by castles and towering rocks, where myth and history mingle inextricably with the Nibelungs (see p. 16), medieval war and piracy, and romantic idylls.  *next page*

The dreams begin 6 kilometres south of Koblenz, on Route 9 along the left bank, at **Stolzenfels,** high above the river. Friedrich Wilhelm IV of Prussia started rebuilding the 14th-century castle, sacked by the French in 1689, at the height of the German Romantic movement when the nation was lovingly reconstructing its past. His Koblenz architects gave it the full treatment—turrets and crenellated battlements, funny little arches, giddy external staircases leading nowhere in particular, half-hidden rose-windows under knobby min-

Down the Rhine west side

arets—all integrated into a fairytale "natural" setting of paths winding past gurgling brooks, of waterfalls among the pine trees, and shrubbery to break the fall of anyone accidentally cast into the dry moat.

From this Romantic pastiche, you plunge into the real Middle Ages at **Rhens,** with its old imperial traditions and authentic Gothic timber-framed houses. The best of these are the old Rathaus (Town Hall) and the Deutschherrenhaus (House of the Knights of the Teutonic Order), directly overlooking the Rhine. Rhens had a special significance as the junction of the fiefdoms of Cologne, Trier, Mainz and the Palatinate—four of the seven electors who chose the Holy Roman Emperor. As such, it served as the meeting-place for their deliberations and the subsequent election of a new ruler. The original Königsstuhl (King's Throne) was erected by Emperor Karl IV at the end of the 14th century. The stone replica that marks the spot was commissioned by Friedrich Wilhelm IV of Prussia.

From here the vines begin, inviting you to the smiling town of **Boppard.** You can walk along its tree-lined Rheinallee, and industry and government are suddenly a million miles away. Stop off at the Karmeliterkirche to enjoy the Renaissance decoration of its interior, particularly the choir stalls and a monumental tomb plaque to Margarete von Eltz.

As you continue on to St. Goar, spare a kind thought for the little Burg Thurnberg on the other side of the river. Better known as **Burg Maus** (Mouse), it is coupled in the popular imagination with the **Burg Katz** (Cat) further south, directly opposite St. Goar. Katz was built at the end of the 14th century by Count Johann von Katzenelnbogen to snatch away the river-tolls that previously went to Maus. **St. Goar** itself has a splendid castle ruin, the **Burg Rheinfels,** built by an earlier—equally rapacious—Katzenelnbogen in 1245. Louis XIV's troops' rampage through the Rhineland left it unscathed, but in 1797 more French troops reduced it to the picturesque ruin you see today. The best vantage point is the clock-tower, from which you can see the extent of this once enormous fortress and the valley it commanded below. (Across the river, the great rock of Lorelei, described on p. 57.)

This was the formidable fortress of the Count Katzenelnbogen.

With the remains of its ivy-covered turreted ramparts remarkably well preserved, **Oberwesel** is a pretty little town. It's framed between two churches — Liebfrauenkirche and Martinskirche, known respectively as the "red" and the "white" churches. The Martinskirche houses some fine Gothic altar-triptychs. The red of the Liebfrauenkirche's sandstone may have been a little overdone in the restoration, but the interior is worth a visit for the superb sculpted Gothic choir-screen and the elaborate high altar. Towering protectively over the whole town is the powerful 12th-century Schönburg castle, now a hotel.

Opposite Kaub, in the middle of the river, you'll see the castle of **Pfalzgrafenstein,** built on an island by Ludwig the Bavarian in 1327 to enforce his right to collect tolls from passing merchant ships. The pentagonal central tower is Ludwig's, the hexagonal outer wall is late Gothic.

A 13th-century German scholar suggested that **Bacharach's** name was derived from the Latin *Bacchi ara*, altar of Bacchus. Modern etymologists are not satisfied, but visitors to this enchanting wine village are soon convinced the old sage was right. The place has an air of unassailable peace and joy with its flower-decorated houses, especially attractive around the market place. Bacharach has earned this peace after a long history of siege and invasion (see p. 22). Look up at the elegant Gothic ruin of the **Wernerkapelle** on a slope above the town. The chapel was built to commemorate the death of a boy named Werner in 1287, at a time when superstitious bigotry encouraged the belief that he had been ritually murdered by the Jews. French troops, landslides and even an earthquake have turned the chapel into a romantic windowless shell, overgrown with wild flowers and shrubbery.

The last part of the left bank itinerary takes you to Bingen past the fanciful 19th-century reconstruction of old medieval castles at Sooneck, once the redoubt of a 13th-century robber-baron, Reichenstein, now a hotel, and **Rheinstein,** worth a visit for its collection of old weapons and armour. As you turn east on the bend in the Rhine at BINGERBRÜCK, look out into the river at the old customs-post, the **Mäuseturm**

Everything, even the post office, is romantic in Bacharach am Rhein.

54

Of Mice and Men

The 9th-century archbishop Hatto of Mainz showed little compassion for his starving flock. He locked up the most importunate of the begging multitude in a barn and set fire to it. "Listen to the squeals of my little mice", he said as he walked back to his palace. The fire killed the beggars but also drove out thousands of mice from the hay and into the archbishop's palace. Hateful Hatto fled to the tower in the middle of the river, but the mice swam after him and gobbled him up.

(Mouse Tower), painted a rather garish yellow. It's notorious for the gruesome legend surrounding the end of a prince of the church. up the Rhine east

The best thing about **Bingen** is its vineyards sloping back behind the town. Try the local wine before boarding the ferry across to Rüdesheim (or take the bridge near GAULSHEIM) to explore the Rhine's right bank.

Before continuing east to Wiesbaden and Mainz, you should complete your valley itinerary by doubling back north from Rüdesheim at least as far as St. Goarshausen. You'll find the slopes on this side are wilder and steeper, less touched by man and his architecture, and you'll have a pano-

ramic view of the castles and churches you saw up close on the left bank.

Rüdesheim is perhaps the best-known of the Rhineland's wine-villages. Certainly its **Drosselgasse** has the liveliest collection of taverns and wine-cellars in the region. Here, in an atmosphere of perpetual festivity, you can try the Rheingau's famous Rieslings, the sparkling *Sekt* and the locally distilled brandies. Find out how it's all done in the national wine museum in the Brömserburg castle. World War II bombardments destroyed most of the original Gothic and Renaissance timber-framed houses, but the reconstructions are quite faithful replicas. The best surviving authentic example of the town's architecture is the 15th- and 16th-century **Brömserhof,** richly decorated with hunting scenes and coats of arms of the local nobility.

Make a side-trip up to the NIEDERWALD to visit the **Germania** monument. Nobody would claim this 35-foot statue was beautiful but the good Germanic lady brandishing the national crown definitely inspires awe and is an amusing example of the extravagances of 19th-century nationalism. The monument was erected in 1883 to celebrate the unification of Germany following the defeat of France in the war of 1870–71. The terrace is a nice place for a picnic with a good view of the valley.

Continue on down to **Assmannshausen,** where you can sample one of the few good red wines of the Rhineland. People suffering from rheumatism or lumbago come here for the warm bromide of lithium waters at the Kurhaus.

On your way to Lorch, look back across the Rhine. Those reconstructed castles of Rheinstein, Reichstein and Sooneck will look much more romantic at this distance. **Lorch** itself has an attractive Gothic church, St. Martin, notable for its 15th-century high altar, carved choir-stalls and a Crucifixion from the 13th century.

Kaub (or *Cuba* in Latin) rates a footnote in European history as the point at which General Blücher took his Silesian Army across the ice-covered Rhine on New Year's Day, 1814, opening up a front from Koblenz to Mannheim to pursue Napoleon into France. A statue of the old warrior, future co-victor at Waterloo, stands on the Kaub quayside pointing to the place where the troops crossed. The town has a Blücher Museum of campaign memorabilia at his old head-

quarters, Metzgergasse 6. The Gutenfels castle above Kaub was one of the three fortresses (with Pfalzgrafenstein in the middle of the river and Bacharach's Stahleck) that sealed the old northern frontier of the Palatinate in the days before German unification.

The road north of Kaub plunges you into the most dramatically soaring part of the Rhine Valley. If you make this stretch of the journey in the late afternoon when a low sun will cast the appropriately romantic shadows, you can dream your way back to the golden mysteries of the Rhine's Middle Ages. As the river turns east towards ST. GOARSHAUSEN, you begin the climb up towards the **Lorelei.** Leave the river road and take the winding route up to the myth-laden rock of the siren that inspired Heinrich Heine's celebrated poem. Good timing should bring you up to her ledge in the evening sunshine described by Heine. You can enjoy the astounding view down the rugged tree-covered cliff and over the swiftly flowing waters towards Oberwesel and the Schönburg castle. Don't despair if it's misty or even raining. The melancholy effect that a drizzle spreads across the valley is worth another poem. **57**

Unhappy Heinrich

*Ich weiss nicht, was soll
    es bedeuten,
Dass ich so traurig bin;
Ein Märchen aus alten Zeiten,
Das kommt mir nicht aus dem
    Sinn.*

He was 26 when he wrote his poem of the Lorelei legend, 26 and hopelessly in love. Jilted by his cousin Amalia, he then fell for her sister Therese, with equal lack of success. The "Lorelei" was one of dozens of poems into which he poured his despair, half-suicidal, half-ironic. No question that the beautiful siren with the golden hair, golden comb and golden necklace was his cruel, beloved Therese. And the poor woeful sailor in his little boat, blindly entranced by her song and dashed to death on the rocks below, was Heinrich Heine.

🏃 The Rheingau

Back at Rüdesheim, you can start your journey through the Rheingau wine country in earnest with a visit to **Johannisberg** to taste the excellent wines in the castle's cellars. Following the 1815 Congress of Vienna that partitioned Napoleon's empire, the castle was handed over to the Habsburgs who made a present of it to Metter-

nich for his efforts on behalf of the old monarchies. With a little proviso: the Habsburgs were to receive each year part of the revenues from the wine-harvest. The castle still belongs to the Metternich family, and the Habsburgs still get their share of the wine profits.

The riverside villages of **Geisenheim, Oestrich-Winkel** and **Eltville** are delightful places to stroll through, both for their charming old and not so old timber-frame houses and ven-

erable and not so venerable wine cellars.

But the jewel of the Rheingau is the former **Kloster Eberbach,** one of the best preserved monasteries in Germany, set back in a valley at the southern edge of the Taunus. The intriguing paradox of Eberbach was the ability of the Cistercian monks to combine the strictest spiritual asceticism with a mastery of the most refined techniques of wine-growing. After the Romans had introduced

This was the view the maiden had from her Lorelei rock as she sang her song to doomed sailors below.

the grape, it was the Eberbach monks who were the veritable founders of the modern wine industry in Germany. Though long since secularized, the abbey still produces some of Rheingau's best wines. The 12th-century abbey church has an austere splendour, resolute- **59** ly Romanesque in spirit despite the Gothic and Baroque additions of later centuries. Its interior is at once bright and cool, with only a few Gothic tombstones for decoration. The cloister and the long double-aisled dormitory still convey a feeling of the tranquillity of the past. Be sure to visit the wine cellars and refectory to see the marvellous collection of old decorative wine-presses, a gentle smile amid the general sobriety of the monastery.

Wiesbaden
Pop. 272,000

The ideal base for your excursions into the Taunus forest and mountains (see below), Wiesbaden is also a good place to rest up after a strenuous journey through the Rhine Valley. The waters of the Kaiser-Friedrich-Bad are excellent for an aching back or chronic sore feet. The capital of the province of Hesse and formerly of the Duchy of Nassau enjoyed its golden era as a fash-

The well-preserved monastery of Eberbach, a masterpiece of Cistercian architecture, is the place where the German wine industry got its start.

ionable spa-resort in the 18th and 19th centuries, culminating in the *belle époque* before World War I. Royalty mingled with the captains of industry in the town's casino and Kurhaus and along the elegant Wilhelmstrasse. This was the world in which novelist Thomas Mann's endearing scoundrel Felix Krull learned the ignoble art of confidence trickery.

The **Wilhelmstrasse** has adapted to the modern world with chic boutiques and the most elegant of Hesse's gentry. At the southern end is the **Städtisches Museum** (municipal museum) with German artists well represented—Lucas Cranach and Bartel Bruyn from the 16th century, Arnold Böcklin (a Swiss) and Oswald Achenbach from the 19th, and Max Beckmann, Lovis Corinth, Max Liebermann and the Russian Alexey Jawlensky from the 20th. On the right as you walk up to the Staatstheater, are superb gardens with the unpoetic name, Warmer-Damm-Anlage. Beyond the theatre is the **Brunnenkolonnade** (colonnade of springs) and **Kurhaus,** if you feel like taking the waters or trying your hand at roulette or baccarat in the casino. East of the Kurhaus is the beautiful **Kurpark** which takes you into another dreamworld with its open-air concerts, delightful beds of flowers and shrubs, beyond which, a walk of about half an hour, is the lovely, restful Rambach valley.

The Taunus

North of Wiesbaden lies the Taunus mountain range, bounded by the rivers Main, Lahn and Rhine—the perfect place to indulge the old German romantic passion for *Waldeinsamkeit*, the simple joy of being alone in the middle of a dense forest.

Head first for TAUNUSSTEIN, following the scenic route **61**

Kurt Röhrig, Frankfurt

Gateway to Germany

Many visitors reach the Rhineland via **Frankfurt,** the financial capital of modern Germany. The war reduced the town to rubble but reconstruction after 1945 was amazingly rapid and efficient, creating out of the ruins a dynamic and prosperous metropolis of 632,000.

Don't miss the superb art collection in the **Städelsches Kunstinstitut,** named after the wealthy 19th-century benefactor J.F. Städel. Among German masterworks, the most important are Dürer's *Job Tended by his Wife* and his portrait of *Katharina Fürleger,* Cranach's altarpiece of the *Holy Family* and Stephan Lochner's *Martyrdom of the Apostles.*

A valiant effort has been made to restore the old **Römerberg** square around the graceful 15th-century façade of the city hall, **Römer,** where German emperors celebrated their coronation. It all looks almost right—the famous gabled silhouette has been painstakingly rebuilt—but inevitably it's a little too shiny bright, a brilliant, rather soulless imitation. The city where Goethe was born (in 1749) has been more successful with its restoration of the **Goethe-haus,** Grosser Hirschgraben 23.

through undulating, wooded countryside. Then proceed on to **Idstein,** a treasured home of the princes of Nassau with wonderfully unspoilt half-timbered houses. Take the road over to ESCH and then down to GLASHÜTTEN, a pretty village where you can leave the car to walk off into the thick forest all around.

Königstein is well worth a visit; part of its ruined fortress dates back to the 5th century. For a stunning view of the Königstein (and even Frankfurt), make a detour north to climb the **Grosser Feldberg,** highest point in the Taunus (3,000 feet). Looking north from the summit, you have a panorama of the Lahn Valley.

The charming village of OBERURSEL is on the way to **Bad Homburg,** a sleepy little spa-resort. This was once the home of Prince Friedrich II of Nassau, the hero of dramatist Heinrich von Kleist's *Prinz von Homburg.* The great days of Bad Homburg's 19th-century brilliance as a casino-town, run by Monte Carlo's wizard François Blanc, have left a dim but graceful echo and you can still lose a fortune here in style. With what's left, stop off in Frankfurt (see box) or take the *Autobahn* directly back to Wiesbaden.

Mainz

If the Rhineland has a reputation for being cheerful, Mainz must take much of the credit. In the course of its years, the town has been a key part of the Roman Empire's northern defences, an indispensable element in the Vatican's control of Catholic Europe, a major commercial centre in the Middle Ages and a focus of intellectual ferment in the revolutionary times of more recent days. Not a lot of laughs in that area. But through it all, the city known as Golden Mainz has always been good for a chuckle, a place where the Carnival's a little crazier and the people's grin a

little broader—in the face of countless invasions and wars. And none was more destructive than the last, World War II, which spared only one out of every five buildings. The reconstruction was slow and painful. But today the town is thriving again, the citizens prosperous, lively, and cheerful.

There are three things to remember about Mainz: its old name *Moguntiacum* comes from the Celtic *Mogo,* god of light; it's the home of Johannes Gutenberg, who spread the good word with his magic printing press; and it made its fortune as the trading centre

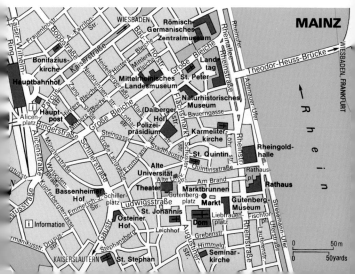

for the wines of the Rhineland—and still does.

Like Cologne, Mainz begins at its **Dom,** in this case a cathedral that uncannily epitomizes the character of the town and its people—plump, ruddy-complexioned and, despite its massive proportions, somehow cosy and intimate. Typically for the Rhineland, the Romanesque basilica has a choir at either end, each with a majestic tower: on the east the austerely simple construction of the 12th century and on the west a more ornate synthesis of Romanesque, Gothic and Baroque which evolved over the 12th to 18th centuries. You get the best overall view from the Leichhof (old cemetery) southwest of the church. The harmony of the complex structure seems the best possible expression of the city's enduring spirit.

But it's not been easy to preserve. A huge fire started by lightning in 1767, French shelling in 1793 and subsequent plundering led to the horrifying decision to auction the whole thing off piece by piece. At the last minute, Bishop Josef Colmar successfully re-

Mainz takes joy in its colourful flower market and great pride in the printing press of Gutenberg.

versed the decision. The withering of age continued to ravage the cathedral and then World War II bombing almost finished it off. Subsequent reconstruction has been nothing short of heroic, though the interior has been stripped of much of its old riches.

Nonetheless there are still some splendid works of art to be seen. The cathedral's lasting treasures are its 29 monumental **tombstones** honouring archbishops of Mainz (45 in all are buried in the cathedral). Enter by the 13th-century Marktportal, with its thousand-year-old bronze Willigis doors. The most important of the tombstones include two late-Gothic sculptures of archbishops Konrad von Daun and Johann von Nassau at the eastern end of the nave, and three 16th-century sculptures—acknowledged masterpieces of the genre—of archbishops Uriel von Gemmingen, Jakob von Liebenstein and Berthold von Henneberg, at the western end of the nave. Note the elegant rococo stalls in the west choir, carved by Franz Anton Hermann. The St. Magnus chapel (to the left of the east altar) contains a superb late-15th-century group sculpture of the *Grablegung* (Burial of Christ).

The **Dommuseum** (cathedral

museum) is also worth a visit for some excellent statuary that has been salvaged over the centuries, in particular 13th-century pieces from the cathedral's choir-screen. Look for the statue of one of the architects, plainly groaning with an aching back from having to serve as a pillar for a doorway. **65**

North of the cathedral on the lively market square is a magnificent Renaissance fountain, the **Marktbrunnen** (1526), the oldest of its kind in Germany. It commemorated the victory of Emperor Karl V over the French at Pavia.

The **Gutenberg Museum** is on the Liebfrauenplatz, east of the cathedral, a neatly designed modern building adjoining and incorporating the fine old 17th-century inn, Zum Römischen Kaiser. Since 1962 it has been the World Museum of the Art of Printing *(Weltmuseum der Druckkunst)*. It presents a fascinating history of men's efforts to communicate with each other in writing, from the most primitive stone and papyrus to today's sophisticated technology of mass-communication. Gutenberg's workshop has been imaginatively reconstructed and there is also one of his original bibles.

You can still get a feel for the old town of Mainz walking

around inside the rectangle leading from the cathedral along Ludwigsstrasse, north on Schillerstrasse and around to the river on the Grosse Bleiche. Seek out the fine 18th-century baroque **Dalberger Hof,** on the Klarastrasse, now the main police station. Other elegant buildings include the Bassenheimer Hof, on the Schillerstrasse, and the Osteiner Hof on the Schillerplatz. Mainz has not lost touch with its golden past.

Excursions

Mosel

In contrast to the Rhine Valley, which mixes its charms with a faint air of melancholy and even a hint of menace, the Mosel is nothing but light and cheer, a carefree winding valley where a mean old Nibelung would be chased away with laughter. The river itself is narrow, and much more amenable than the Rhine, the countryside gentler, less dramatic. Mosel wines stand proudly beside those of the Rhine and indeed there are many Frenchmen who are happier with the Mosels because of their affinity with the wines of Alsace.

If your time is limited, it's best to take Autobahn 48 west from Koblenz for 30 kilometres before cutting down to Cochem to drive along the river road (49 and 53) as far as Bernkastel, in the most attractive and most typical part of the Mosel's pleasant green valley. From Bernkastel you go on to visit Trier before heading

There is nothing more restful than the gentle landscape of the Mosel. **67**

back towards Manderscheid to explore a little of the Eifel plateau.

If you're not in a hurry, follow the river road from Koblenz to MOSELKERN, where you turn off to visit the **Burg Eltz,** a fairytale castle piled piece upon piece between the 12th and 16th centuries in an enchanting conglomeration of all the fantasies anyone ever had about castles—towers, soaring granite walls, turrets and half-timbered gables and look-outs tucked away where you would least expect them. Perched on a hill above the babbling Eltzbach stream, this fortress cannot fail to make you smile rather than shiver— the very essence of the Mosel's good nature.

In **Cochem** you can take the chair-lift up the Pinnerkreuz hill for a view of the sleepy little town with its restored castle. From Cochem the valley winds lazily round to **Beilstein** with its 16th-century *Fachwerk- häuser* (timber-framed houses). Metternich was the last owner of the castle ruins here, which the French forces of 1689 had left with scarcely more than the pentagonal belfry and an arched doorway high above the ground.

On the left bank as you approach ZELL is the graceful ruin of the 12th-century **Marienburg** convent, closed in the 16th century because the archbishop of Trier disapproved of the nuns' unseemly behaviour. It was destroyed during the Thirty Years' War in successive occupation by the Bavarians, Swedes and French. The French came back in 1792 to finish it off. The convent enjoys a lovely view of the valley and the rolling vineyards.

Bernkastel-Kues is a picture-book wine village—actually twin villages on either side of the river. Its wines are justly famed and the half-timbered taverns you drink them in charming, especially on the Römerstrasse, though sometimes a little over-done. For serious tasting, seek out the wine cellars. The **Markt** on the Bernkastel side of the river is a popular focus of town life, notable for its fountain depicting the angel Michael, patron saint of Bernkastel. It was built in 1606, two years before the fine town hall overlooking it. The most bizarre of the old timber-frame houses, just off the market place, is the top-heavy **Spitzhaus** (Pointed House),

Local citizens take great pains to keep tiny Trittenheim shipshape.

built in 1583, a triumph of will-power over structural stability.

After Bernkastel you can continue on the river road or backtrack to the *Autobahn* to go on to Trier.

Trier

Not content with being Germany's oldest city, Trier proudly proclaims that it is even older than Rome. A house on the market-place bears the inscription: *Ante Romam Treveris stetit annis mille trecentis* (Trier was standing 1,300 years before Rome). But historians dismiss the claim that Trier was founded by Trebeta, son-in-law of the Assyrian queen Semiramis, as a legend invented to boost the town's image in the early Middle Ages. Already a major settlement of the Celtic Treveri when Augustus built a provincial capital—Augusta Treverorum—in 15 B.C., Trier was a favourite home away from home for numerous Roman emperors in the 3rd and

4th centuries A.D. Constantine I, the first Christian emperor, spent the early years of his reign here. Acquiring a bishop around 315, Trier became Germany's earliest Christian centre and has been a stronghold of Catholicism ever since.

There is definitely something sunny and Mediterranean about Trier, sitting comfortably in the Mosel valley plain, encouraging an easy-going way of life that has maintained itself without too much difficulty to the present. Nowadays the town thrives as the centre of the Mosel wine-trade and enjoys unspectacular but satisfactory prosperity by not encouraging heavy—dirty—industry. The light-hearted ambiance is greatly enhanced by the presence of 2,500 students at the newly re-established university.

Despite the usual ravages of war and time, the town's Roman origins are remarkably visible, the basic urban ground-plan unchanged for nearly 2,000 years. You still approach the town centre through the powerful **Porta Nigra** (Black Gate). Standing at the north end of town to face the road leading to the Rhine, you can see that it was built to resist the ancient Germanic hordes—and its massive proportions guaranteed that it did. Dating from the 2nd century A.D., its sandstone blocks were joined not by mortar but by iron clamps. The name Porta Nigra is a post-Roman reference to the pollution of the ages, but at the base you can see that the gate was once pale pink.

In 1028 the Syrian monk Simeon came to Trier on a pilgrimage from Jerusalem and shut himself up in a cell inside the gate's walls until his death a few years later. The archbishop of Trier honoured him by transforming part of the structure into a church, the **Simeonsstift.** Its superb two-storey cloister now houses the municipal museum and tourist information centre. The ground-floor archways of the cloister are a magnificent combination of white limestone and red sandstone, lending solid support to the elegant arcade of the upper storey. The museum has some admirable 15th–18th-century ecclesiastical sculpture, the best of which are perhaps the statues of Saints Helen, James, Peter and Paul from the old Steipe (the town's 15th-century hall of festivities, reconstructed after war

Rowing competitions on the Mosel attract oarsmen from all over.

Trier's Porta Nigra—Black Gate— was pink when the Romans erected it. It's still the way into town.

damage at the western corner of the market place). You might also be interested in the iron *Schandmasken* (masks of shame), which wrongdoers had to wear on the medieval pillory on the market-place.

Walking south on Simeon-strasse, you'll pass on the left (No. 19) the rather too garishly renovated but still graceful 13th-century **Dreikönigenhaus** (House of the Three Kings). In the old days the front door was on the second storey, reached by a staircase that could be removed in case of danger.

The **Hauptmarkt** is in every sense the heart of Trier, a lively centre with cheerful merchants around the Petrusbrunnen (St. Peter's Fountain) that proclaims the sturdy cardinal virtues of Wisdom, Justice,

and fortress-like, a powerful Romanesque structure that symbolizes the town's former functions as a bastion of the Roman Empire (pagan and holy) and a centre of the Christian church. The two most important works of art inside are by sculptor Hans Ruprecht Hoffmann, designer of the Petrusbrunnen. They are the **pulpit,** 1572, and the **Allerheiligenaltar** (All Saints' Altar), 1614, on the south side of the church.

The other church worth visiting is the adjoining **Liebfrauenkirche,** a sober, imposing 13th-century Gothic building whose floor-plan describes a 12-petal rose, the mystic flower, symbol of the Virgin Mary. The simple design creates an immensely reposing interior.

After a pleasant stroll through the French-style gardens of the restored Renaissance Kurfürstliches Palais (Elector's Palace), you're back in ancient Roman Trier. It's a good idea to begin your orientation at the excellent **Landesmuseum,** Ostallee, with its wonderfully lucid presentation of Roman art and artefacts, probably the best in Germany. The **Kaiserthermen** (Imperial Baths) date from the early 4th century A.D. At the eastern end is the miraculously pre-

Moderation and Strength. These are the qualities that speak from the stones of the Renaissance and baroque houses surrounding the square, badly damaged in the wars but lovingly reconstructed. The square is dominated on the south side by the solid tower of the 15th-century St. Gangolf church. You get to it through a fine baroque archway between the houses.

Trier's **Dom,** one of Germany's oldest churches, is massive

served *caldarium* or hot baths, a hall originally measuring 121 by 66 feet. To the west was a domed *tepidarium* and a *frigidarium* with five swimming pools, next to a dressing-room, massage-parlour and steam bath. At the other end of the Kaiserstrasse, turn left on Friedrich-Wilhelm-Strasse to

The wide open spaces of the Eifel offer plenty of opportunities to stretch your legs on a good hike.

the cosier **Barbarathermen,** 200 years older than the Imperial Baths. It's nicely overgrown with moss, grass, ivy and wild flowers. At the Mosel you can see the Römerbrücke (Roman Bridge), 18th-century arches on 2nd-century pillars.

Leading from the bridge, the Karl-Marx-Strasse—a very rare street name in West Germany—takes you directly into Brückenstrasse to No. 10, birthplace of this Catholic town's most famous and very uncatholic son. Surrounded by topless bars and cabarets, the **Karl-Marx-Haus** is a fascinating collection of memorabilia of the author of *Das Kapital*—exhibited here in manuscript—and co-author with Friedrich Engels of the *Communist Manifesto*. Photos show the young Marx with all the great revolutionaries of his day. Just as we've been led to expect of good revolutionaries, the house turns out to be a nice bourgeois home.

Eifel

You can take the *Autobahn* towards Koblenz and turn off at WITTLICH for a little sortie into the Eifel plateau and its volcanoes. The drive will lead you first through gentle green countryside of rolling hills to **Manderscheid** on the swiftly flowing river Lieser. At the edge of dense forest, the town is dominated by the ruins of two fortresses known simply as the Oberburg (Upper Castle) and Niederburg (Lower Castle),

the latter looking down into the narrow Lieser valley. Between Manderscheid and ECKFELD you can take a marvellous walk (45 minutes) up to the **belvedere** which commands a perfect view of the Lieser valley and the two castle ruins. Four kilometres west of Manderscheid, you may be interested in making the hour's hike up the **Mosenberg** volcano, with its four extinct craters.

The road between Manderscheid and DAUN passes some volcanic lakes known as *Maare*—Holz, Pulver (the prettiest), Schalkenmehrener, Weinfelder and Gemündener. *Maare*, caused by explosions through the earth's surface of gas without lava, are hollows surrounded by a ridge of cinders, all more or less round in shape and filled with water. From Daun the route winds through pine forests and meadowland to ULMEN and the *Autobahn* back to Koblenz.

As an alternate route from Trier to Koblenz, leave the *Autobahn* at KIRSCH and drive south-east to pick up the Hunsrück-Höhenstrasse (route 327) near THALFANG. This picturesque route takes you back to Koblenz through the lovely **Hunsrück** hills and **Idarwald** forest via MORBACH, KASTEL-LAUN and Boppard.

Heidelberg and Worms

Heidelberg is one of the most enjoyable towns in Germany, at least in part because of its university, dating back to 1386, with students whose verve is legendary. In this town, the scholars have always drunk a lot, duelled a little and, when necessary, done an amazing amount of serious academic work. It has been a poet's delight, a cradle of the German Romantic movement. Situated at the western end of the lovely Neckar Valley, the old capital of the Palatinate has survived its strife-ridden history to offer visitors a haven of pure pleasure.

Americans have long had a special affinity for the town. It is said that this is why Heidelberg was not bombed in 1945. It had already been singled out as headquarters for the U.S. Army at the end of the war.

The **castle** was ravaged by the troops of Louis XIV in 1689 and 1693. Yet, visiting these remains from the 14th to 17th centuries certainly proves to be more of an adventure than a tour of a perfectly preserved castle. The terrace and the various look-outs, especially the **Rondell** on the west side, command an enchanting view of the castle gardens, the old city and the wooded slopes of the Neckar Valley.

The styles span 500 years of architecture. In the north-east corner you can compare the Italian Renaissance style of the **Gläserner Saalbau** (Hall of Mirrors), 1549, and the later German Renaissance **Otthein-richsbau.** The statuary in the niches of the early 17th-century **Friedrichsbau**'s façade represent the various members of the old Wittelsbach family who provided the Electors Palatine—the originals can be seen in the castle museum.

Good guided tours are conducted in English and German, but you can visit the exterior by yourself. Particularly worthwhile are the castle **gardens** through the Elisabethentor, named after the English Princess Elizabeth Stuart, wife of Friedrich V of the Palatinate.

The most amusing part of the interior is the **Fassbau** (Barrel Wing), specially constructed to hold two gigantic wine-barrels. The 1751 barrel holds 221,726 litres, the 1662 barrel, a mere 45,000. The guardian of the barrels at one time was a dwarf named Perkeo, who had been a court-jester of the Medici in Florence in the 18th century. He was said to have drunk 10 to 12 litres of wine a day and lived to the age of 83—dying after drinking a glass of water.

Heidelberg's city-centre retains some of its 17th-century atmosphere around the Marktplatz, thanks in large part to the exclusion of car traffic. The Heiliggeistkirche (Church of the Holy Ghost) on the square is notable mainly for the little shops and stalls that still cling to its walls. Opposite, at Hauptstrasse 178, is the fine Renaissance house **Zum Ritter,** built in 1592. The town's taverns are as lively as ever, for students from 18 to 88.

The **Kurpfälzisches Museum** (Palatinate Museum), Hauptstrasse 97, has some admirable 15th-century art from the Rhineland and southern Germany; its prize piece—Tilman Riemenschneider's wooden sculpture of the **Zwölfboten-altar** (Altar of the Twelve Apostles). There's also a very good collection of the work of German Expressionist Emil Nolde. The museum exhibits an excellent replica of Homo Heidelbergensis or rather his 500,000-year-old jawbone. (The original can be seen at the university's geological department, Im Neuenheimer Feld 234.)

The **university,** on Universitätsplatz and Augustinergasse, along with the attractive new extensions along the right bank of the Neckar, has always been known for a mixture of earnest scholarship and good fun. Its great scholars have included sociologist Max Weber, physiologist Hermann von Helmholtz, physicist Robert Kirchhoff and his more famous colleague Robert Bunsen (1811–99), known for the burner used in all laboratory experiments, the forerunner of the modern gas-stove.

In Heidelberg's antique shops you will see prized examples of Biedermeier, the heavy 19th-century furniture ostensibly named after "the great Philistine poet" Gottlieb Biedermaier. In fact, the personnage was invented (*bieder* means "ingenuous") at the University of Heidelberg by Adolf Kussmaul and poet Ludwig Eichrodt to satirize the insensitive materialism of the times. For lesser crimes, students were thrown into the **Karzer** or student prison, which can still be visited at Augustinergasse 2.

For a tranquil moment away from the town's bustle, walk along the right bank of the river Neckar. Take the **Philosophenweg** (Philosophers' Path) through a garden and uphill to the Heiligenberg. You'll pass another garden dedicated to poet Friedrich Hölderlin and easily understand, as you look around the peaceful valley, why Heidelberg attracted the German Romantics.

Before going north again, stop off at **Speyer** to see its magnificent 11th-century Romanesque **Dom** (cathedral), with its noble silhouette of four towers and two domes. The Kaisergruft (Imperial Mausoleum) is quite awe-inspiring in its proportions and intricate vaulting among the 20 pillars. The monumental tombstone of Rudolf von Habsburg stands at the entrance to the resting-place of eight German emperors and kings.

Halfway on the road back to Mainz, the town of **Worms** is a veritable crossroads of the three spiritual persuasions that have marked Germany's history. Catholicism has reigned there since the 6th century and the **cathedral** *(Dom)* is one of the Rhineland's major Romanesque and Gothic edifices. Particularly beautiful is the 12th-century sculpture of *Thronender Christus* (Christ Sitting in Judgement) inside the south doorway. There is a fine 18th-century baroque altar by Balthasar Neumann.

Buried in Speyer's cathedral are eight German emperors and kings.

Jews made their home in Worms in the 11th century and built their **synagogue** there at the south-west corner of town in 1034, the oldest stone-built synagogue in Europe. The great scholar Rabbi Raschi founded his Yeshiva school, and the Jewish community of Worms, 30 per cent of the city's population, enjoyed its golden age. The synagogue, coupled with a women's ritual bath, was destroyed over and over again by the local citizenry (see pp. 17–18). Each time, it was rebuilt; most recently as it had been in 1700 with much of the original masonry. It serves as a small museum.

Protestantism holds a proud place in Worms with the **Lutherdenkmal** (Luther Monument), celebrating Martin Luther's triumpant confrontation with the Catholic Church at the Diet of Worms in 1521 (see p. 19). The 19th-century monument shows Luther surrounded by other heroic rebels of the Church, including John Wycliffe of England, Jan Hus of Czechoslovakia and Girolamo Savonarola of Italy.

Worms also pays a little **79**

homage to paganism at the Nibelungenbrücke, where a statue of Hagen is shown throwing the Nibelungs' treasure into the Rhine, precipitating the adventure that inspired Richard Wagner's operas (see p. 16). And if you've ever wondered where the name of the Rhine wine Liebfraumilch came from, it's Worms' 15th-century church, Liebfrauenkirche, on the north side of town, still surrounded by its valued vineyards.

Hebrew lettering on the tombs— one of the last remnants of the great Jewish community of Worms.

Düsseldorf
Pop. 620,000

Though the Rhineland as a whole does not lay claim to chic and sophistication, Düsseldorf comes closest. The city suffered badly in World War II, but has rebuilt with great self-confidence and sustains an airy cosmopolitanism. The girls walking along the famous Königsallee have a spring in their step and a sparkle in their eye to stand fair comparison with those on the Champs-Elysées and Fifth Avenue.

The **Königsallee** is a masterpiece of urban elegance. The wide, long straight avenue has

a fountain and a waterway running down its middle, with swans swimming through the reflection of the chestnut trees on the banks. Built on the area where Napoleon had razed the town's old fortifications, it was originally called Kastanienallee (Chestnut Avenue) until Friedrich-Wilhelm IV of Prussia visited it in the stormy year of 1848. Radicals pelted him with horse manure and the city fathers subsequently sought to make amends by renaming the street Königsallee (King's Avenue). Called simply the "Kö" now, its western side is rather sombre, lined with banks and insurance companies, while the eastern side catches the afternoon sun and is known as the *Schokoladenseite*. This is where you sit on the café-terraces, buy your pastries and chocolates in the dainty shops and your haute-couture in the fashionable boutiques. While you're sipping your coffee on the terrace, don't be surprised to see small boys whirling past, cartwheeling their way along the Kö. They are the town's time-honoured *Radschläger* earning pocket-money from a public they hope is enchanted.

Two local heroes both turned to France for their inspiration but remained resolutely German in expression.

The immensely popular Elector-Palatine Johann Wilhelm II—Jan Wellem to Düsseldorfers—was the epitome at the turn of the 18th century of the Rhenish princes enamoured of the Versailles style of living, which Jan Wellem adapted to his own people's more relaxed good humour. A splendid **equestrian statue** of him stands in the middle of the horseshoe-shaped Marktplatz in the centre of the **Altstadt** (Old Town), where his spirit lives on in lively streets and taverns.

Poet Heinrich Heine (1797–1856) was born in Düsseldorf during the French occupation. Though he absorbed a French culture which subsequently took him to Paris, he never relinquished his melancholy-ironic, German view of the world. He was particularly scornful of the stiffness of the French poetry he had to learn at his Düsseldorf lycée. "I could have died for France," he later wrote, "but compose French verse? Never again!" In the **Hofgarten** there is a charming monument to Heine on the hill known as Napoleonsberg. Appropriately it is crowned by a French sculpture, *Harmonie*, the last work of Aristide Maillol.

The city offers two fine art museums: the **Städtisches**

Kunstmuseum has an impressive collection of the important 19th-century Düsseldorf School—Schadow, Cornelius, Achenbach and Lessing; the **Schloss Jägerhof** houses the Kunstsammlung Nordrhein-Westfalen (North Rhine-Westphalia Art Collection), devoted mainly to the modern masters, including Klee, Braque, Picasso, Kandinsky and Mondrian.

You can see what a good life the Rhenish princes enjoyed in the 18th century by visiting the delightful **Schloss Benrath,** 10 kilometres south of Düsseldorf. The princes' graceful summer residence, designed by Nicolas de Pigage, was originally laid out with geometrically planned French gardens. But 19th-century tastes preferred the English style and the gardens were re-landscaped. They're still a joy.

The Königsallee is to Düsseldorf what Fifth Avenue is to New York.

What to Do

Shopping

Düsseldorf is without a doubt the most attractive shopping centre in the Rhineland, offering top-quality goods in beautifully appointed shops along the Königsallee, Berliner Allee and Schadowstrasse. The fashion boutiques feature all the international couturiers, but if you don't want to pay German prices for French and Italian clothes, look out for the good quality German **leather-** and **sportswear.** Of course, if you want **Eau de Cologne,** the place to go is 47 kilometres south of Düsseldorf.

For children and their parents, you'll find marvellously stocked **toy** shops in every major Rhineland town. The national technical genius has gone into producing the world's best model trains and remote-controlled boats, planes

A Rose by Any Other Name
Eau de Cologne has gone through a series of different names since it was first concocted in 1709 by Johann Maria Farina. Farina called it "Aqua Mirabilis" (wonder water). "Eau de Cologne" was understandably the preferred name during the French occupation, but one competitor dubbed his product "4711", after his new street number under the French régime. With the assertion of German national identity in the 19th century, many opted for "Kölnisch Wasser"—about as romantic to the German ear as "Cologne Water" to the English. Call it what you will, it's still the perfect way to finish a shave or freshen up before an important date.

and helicopters. You can also find superb scale-models, apparently accurate in every detail, of the castles you've been visiting in the Rhine Valley. Some are available either in their present romantically ruined form or in the mint condition of their best days. And of course the appropriate sol-diers can also be obtained in lead, tin or cardboard for you to fight your own Thirty Years' War or other bloodbath of your choice.

For **antiques,** the best bets are in Düsseldorf, Heidelberg, Bonn and, above all, in Cologne's Altstadt (Old Town) around the Gross St. Martin

church. You may stumble on good Romantic landscape painting of the 19th century as well as Biedermeier bookcases and Gothic and Romanesque statuary salvaged from ruined churches.

Chinaware, old Meissen or modern Rosenthal, is of very good quality and design, as are

cutlery, kitchen utensils and electronic **gadgets** for the house if you like utilitarian gifts with style. German **linen** is much appreciated, especially the fa-

Souvenirs of the robust Rhineland humour abound; at market, there's no telling what you might find.

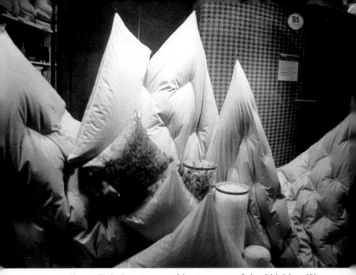

A goose-down Federbett is one of best ways to fight Old Man Winter; after dark, you'll find warmth and good cheer in Rhineland taverns.

mous *Federbett*, the duck- or goose-down Continental quilts that will keep you warm through any energy crisis. Among **precision instruments,** the best buys are binoculars and telescopes and, while the competition from Japan is keen, there are still many fine cameras on the market. Cologne's international Photokina fair is a great opportunity to see the latest technology.

The presence of so many great orchestras and musicians in Germany means that the selection of **records** here is second perhaps only to the United States. **Musical instruments** enjoy a venerable tradition, with the finest harmonicas as well as the leading grand pianos.

Delicatessen, Germany's gift to the hungry, is a souvenir you may well consume before leaving the country. There are the excellent hams, myriad sausages and a few good cheeses, all very well packed for travel. Mosel and Rhine wines (see pp. 95–98) make nice gifts, too.

Entertainment

In a region of such determined party-goers the good times are, as often as not, provided by the people themselves rather than by professional entertainers. The best nights out on the town are spent in taverns singing and dancing with your friends. The liveliest towns are Düsseldorf, Cologne and Heidelberg, but also Trier. Düsseldorf, in addition, offers a more elegant, tailored night-life of discotheques and nightclubs. In Cologne you can have a lively time around the Altstadt neighbourhood taverns and discos, open till the early hours

of the morning on the Salzgasse and Eisenmarkt. Heidelberg throws its student taverns along the Hauptstrasse open to all comers. And Trier's are equally hospitable, if somewhat less boisterous, in the streets off the Hauptmarkt.

As a result of traditions started in the days when each was a capital of a principality eager to make its own cultural mark, Düsseldorf, Cologne, Mainz, Frankfurt and Heidelberg all have excellent **theatre.** Düsseldorf's Schauspielhaus stages some of the finest theatre in Germany and the **opera** at the Deutsche Oper am Rhein is first class. If your German is up **87**

Carnival

The Rhinelanders love an old-fashioned party and by old-fashioned we mean going back centuries. All year round, from the pre-Lenten Carnival, through Easter, Midsummer Night and the autumn wine festivals to St. Martin's Feast in November and finally Christmas, the people welcome any excuse to dress up, dance around and drink a little wine.

The most famous and longest-lasting party is the Carnival, seen at its craziest in Cologne and Mainz, but celebrated throughout the Rhineland with Düsseldorf and Bonn offering their own brand of madness. Traditionally, the festivities are announced at a meeting of all the town's various carnival clubs at 11 minutes past 11 on the 11th day of the 11th month (November), 11 being the madman's lucky number. After this preliminary party, a mild warm-up, so to speak, the revellers break up till the New Year when the round of balls and banquets and masked processions begins in not-too-much earnest. The long winter nights are often brightened by party-goers wandering around the streets in harlequin costumes and other inspired paraphernalia derived from the great Venetian revels of the 18th century.

Every trade and profession worthy of the name—cobblers and doctors, carpenters and lawyers, tailors and computer-salesmen—vie to put on the most ingenious and uproarious ball possible. The climax is the last weekend leading to Shrove Tuesday (Mardi Gras), before all good Catholics settle down to a soberer Lenten existence of (relative) abstinence and seemly behaviour.

The tone is set on the Thursday with Weiberfastnacht (the Women's Carnival) when wives lord it (lady it?) over their husbands and their friends' husbands, dancing and playing with whom they choose and nobody knows or worries who beneath the masks and costumes is married to whom. Friday and Saturday: more parties as the celebration continues with people strolling around town in the most outrageous outfits. Even if someone felt like blushing, you wouldn't be able to tell under all the clown make-up.

Sunday it's the kids' turn to parade through the streets. *Rosenmontag* (Rose Monday) brings the biggest procession of all, with dozens—in Cologne and Mainz, hundreds—of elaborate floats displaying papier-mâché masks of popular and unpopular political figures in invariably undignified postures.

On Tuesday, hung-over, everybody goes back to work. Or, on Wednesday.

to it, try the satirical cabaret at the Kommödchen. Besides its Opernhaus and Schauspielhaus, Cologne has good cabaret-theatre at the Floh de Cologne (Cologne Flea) and Die *M*achtwächter (the *M*ight-Watchmen).

Music is of course a highlight in the Rhineland's calendar and you should look out for programmes of concerts all-year-round in Düsseldorf, Cologne, Frankfurt and at Bonn's Beethovenhalle. Wiesbaden puts on an international music festival in May, and Heidelberg holds concerts in the courtyard of the castle in the summer. From July to September, Koblenz has open-air concerts along the Rhein-anlagen and in the Blumen-hof, but its masterpiece is the floating operetta festival on the Rhine.

Fireworks are a big thing in the Rhineland—perhaps a kind of reminder of the many times the region has gone up in

flames. Heidelberg puts on a spectacular show at its castle on the first Saturday in June, July and September. In the middle of August the Rhine Valley from Koblenz to Braubach is set alight with fireworks. The castles are dramatically illuminated—as if they were burning down yet again.

For those who find it entertaining to win or lose money in the **casino,** the best baccarat and roulette are at Bad Homburg and Wiesbaden.

Sports

Germans are a healthy, sports-loving people and Rhinelanders are no exception, though they're perhaps a bit more relaxed about it. They do provide plenty of outdoor facilities.

If you're a **golf** player, Cologne, Düsseldorf and Frankfurt all have 18-hole courses on the outskirts of town. You'll find **tennis** courts nearly everywhere. And just because you're far from the sea there's no reason not to go **swimming.** Even small Rhineland towns have at least one public pool. At the spa of Bad Honnef across the river south of Bonn, you'll find an open-air mineralized pool where you can exercise and get rid of your ailments at the same time. If you are hardy enough for river swimming, try the Mosel rather than the Rhine.

Sailing regattas are held regularly in the summer on the Rhine at Cologne and Düsseldorf. There is sailing on the Mosel at Trier. **Rowing** is popular at Koblenz and Bonn.

If you prefer peace to excitement try an afternoon's fishing at the river. You might land a big trout. **91**

Camping and **hiking** are especially good in the Taunus and the Eifel (see p. 115). The Taunus also offers some opportunities for novice mountain-climbing. Large towns and nearly all the spa-resorts, such as Wiesbaden, Bad Homburg and Bad Ems, have **riding** facilities. The best riding trails are in the Taunus, but also along the Neckar Valley outside Heidelberg. **Cycling** enthusiasts can hire bikes in many railway stations (see p. 106) and then set off on special trails. A fine way to explore the countryside.

Hunting is of course a favourite German sport. You should get details of season dates, restrictions and availability of game from the tourist office. There's good **fishing** for trout, salmon, eel, carp and perch in the Mosel and in the countless streams feeding the Rhine between Mainz and Koblenz. It's easy to get the obligatory fishing permit from the local municipal authority.

Among spectator sports there is **horse racing** at Wiesbaden, Cologne and Düsseldorf, as well as top level **showjumping** at the Cologne and Düsseldorf tournaments. Cologne also has one of the leading **soccer** teams in Europe and you can see more good football at Frankfurt and Düsseldorf.

Wining and Dining

There's a good life to be had wining and dining in the Rhineland, and a few surprises. You certainly won't go hungry—the portions are if anything too copious—and thirst is easily quenched with good beer and exquisite wines, chased by hearty brandies and *Schnaps.* *

Let's start with **breakfast** *(Frühstück)* because the Germans have their own way of doing this. They'll serve you coffee (stronger than British or American), tea or even hot chocolate. But the main characteristic is the cold meats—ham, salami and liver-sausage —and cheeses served with the bread. And not just one kind of bread. You can get brown (rye, with caraway seeds), rich black (pumpernickel) and white, with or without raisins, all on one plate. If you like boiled eggs, try the *Eier im Glas*, two four-minute eggs served whole, already shelled, in a glass dish. It saves you the trouble of decid-

---

* For a comprehensive guide to wining and dining in Germany, consult the Berlitz EUROPEAN MENU READER.

ing whether to crumble or guillotine the top of your eggshell.

Lunch is often the main meal of the day as Germans like to have a light *Abendbrot* (literally "evening bread")—a slightly more copious version of the breakfast cold meats and cheeses, with the addition of a salad—in place of dinner.

From Soup to Salad
Whichever you choose as your main meal, you may pick up the German habit of starting off with a hearty and warming

If you go in autumn, try the venison, a superb local speciality.

soup—of beans *(Bohnensuppe)*, lentils *(Linsensuppe)* or cabbage *(Kohlsuppe)* often with pieces of sausage in it—or in summer a cold fruit-soup *(Fruchtsuppe)*, made of cherries *(Kirschen)*, strawberries *(Erdbeeren)* or red currants *(Rote Johannisbeeren)* with a tart touch of lemon juice.

The most constant feature of a German meal is some part of the pig. It's said that the only thing they don't use is the squeal. The local ham *(Schinken)* from the Eifel is excellent. Sausage *(Wurst)*, produced in dozens of different varieties, come more or less spiced and garlicked, the mildest being the Frankfurter. Among the more piquant, you'll find the smoked *dürre Runde* of the Taunus. Pigs' hocks *(Schweinshachse* or sometimes *Hämchen* in local dialect) are a great favourite on Saturday nights. And one dish they serve around the Rheingau, *Sulperknochen*, includes the ears, the snout, the tail and the trotters, on a bed of sauerkraut and a purée of peas. Drink what you like, but you're crazy if you don't wash it down with beer.

As you can see, Rhinelanders like robust dishes and there's a whopper called *Himmel und Erde* (Heaven and Earth), which is what it feels like when you plough through this mixture—absolutely delicious, by the way—of apples, blood-sausage and leeks. Hessians have something similar, with potatoes in place of the apples. While on the subject of blood-sausage, a taste—if you don't have it—well worth acquiring, you should know about the dish the people of Cologne laughingly call *Kölsche Kaviar*, in fact, a blood-sausage served with slices of raw onion. Rhinelanders have another trick up their sleeves with *Halve Hahn*, which means "half a chicken" but turns out to be a rye-bread-roll stuffed with hot mustard and Dutch cheese. They love it.

For more delicate palates there are some fine **fish** dishes —salmon *(Lachs)* on the Rhine, terrific with dill, and pike *(Hecht)* or eel *(Aal)* on the Mosel. Don't be scared of the eel. *Moselaal in Riesling* (Mosel eel simmered in Riesling white wine) is one of the great dishes of the Western world.

Gourmets are always impressed by the majestic way in which Rhinelanders prepare their **game**—venison, hare, partridge and woodcock. The venison *(Wildbret)* is usually carefully marinated to a fine degree of tenderness and served with sweet sauces of raisins or red currants or purée of chestnuts. The game birds are treated with similar loving care and presented with a masterful sense of High Kitsch on the tray. Just try a *Hunsrücker Rehkeule*—leg of venison from the deer hunted in the Hunsrück hills—with a well-chilled Piesporter Goldtröpfchen and you may never want to go home.

King and queen of the **vegetables** are naturally the potato and the cabbage. *Bratkartoffeln* (sautéed potatoes) get rather boring after a while, but the *Reibekuchen* (potato pancakes) and potato salad (*Kartoffelsalat*) spiced up with onion and pieces of bacon make excellent variations. Cabbage of course means first and foremost *Sauerkraut*, often beautifully prepared in white wine with juniper berries, caraway seeds and cloves. But there's also the sweet-and-sour red cabbage, *Rotkraut*, done with apples, raisins and white vinegar. And a good green cabbage salad (*Weisskohlsalat*), also with chopped onion and bacon-bits. More aristocratic is the very good white asparagus (*Spargel*). In early summer a whole meal can be prepared around them, French-style with vinaigrette or German-style with ham.

Cheese and Sweets

The only noteworthy native German cheese you're likely to run into is the *Limburger*, a semi-hard cheese spiced with tarragon, caraway, chives or parsley.

And then, there's the pastry *(Gebäck)*, the heavenly concoctions that lure fat old ladies and thin young men into the *Konditorei* (café-cum-pastry-shop) without the slightest trace of guilt. Local specialities include the *Spekulatius* Christmas biscuits, the crumbly *Streuselkuchen* and the myriad joys of marzipan, but let's not be regional. Konditorei-hopping is a national pastime and every Rhineland shop will have *Schwarzwälder Kirschtorte* (Black Forest cherry cake), Viennese *Apfelstrudel* and a dozen other fruit and chocolate and cream cakes to reduce us all to giggling children, diet be damned.

Wine

The wines of the Rhineland and the adjoining Mosel are a delightful adventure, even for spoiled French connoisseurs. Apart from the very respectable reds *(Rotwein)* produced at Assmannshausen and Ahr, the drinkable wines are all white *(Weisswein)*.

To help you around the

labels on the bottles, you should know the most highly reputed are those of the **Rheingau**, between Wiesbaden and Rüdesheim, which benefiting from the bend in the river have slopes facing south to the sun. The pick of the crop are the *Schloss Johannisberger, Hattenheimer, Kloster Eberbacher, Steinberger* and *Rüdesheimer*. The **Rheinhessen** region on the left bank south of Mainz, boasts the *Liebfraumilch* of Worms, along with the great *Niersteiner Domtal* and *Oppenheimer*. Only marginally less impressive among Rhine wines are those of the **Rheinpfalz** (Rhineland-Palatinate) further south on the left bank of the river, especially the *Wachenheimer*, and the **Mittelrhein** wines, from Rüdesheim to Koblenz, where Bingen, Bacharach, Boppard and Oberwesel have nothing to be ashamed of.

The **Mosel** wines, bottled in green glass to distinguish them from the brown Rhine bottles, enjoy their own delicate reputation with the most celebrated being the *Bernkasteler, Piesporter, Graacher* and *Zeltinger*.

Since 1971, the Germans have divided their wines into three categories of ascending quality: *Deutscher Tafelwein*, ordinary table wine; *Qualitäts-*

wein bestimmter Anbaugebiete, a wine certified to be from a specific region; and *Qualitäts-wein mit Prädikat*, corresponding to the French *vin d'appellation contrôlée*, a wine of quality.

The last thing you may notice on a German wine label is the distinction made between the stages at which the wine's grapes, mostly the Riesling variety, were picked. *Kabinett*, the wine from the earliest picked grapes is the lightest and driest of the crop. You'll find *Spätlese*, made from grapes picked later, riper, more full-bodied and often sweeter. *Auslese* wine is richer than the *Spätlese*, coming from a selection of the very ripest grapes picked while others remain on the vine. *Beerenlese* goes a stage further in richness, de-

Without sausages Germany would not be Germany, but keep your palate clear for wine-tasting.

rived from grapes picked one by one in an overripe state. And the ultimate is the *Trockenbeerenauslese*, comparable to France's very best Sauternes and made from grapes that have deliberately been allowed to mould with an enriching fungus.

There are also some very creditable sparkling, champagne-like wines that the Germans call *Sekt*, notably in the Rheingau's Eltville and Hochheim. The latter's vineyard, by the way, is at the origin of the word "hock", the English gentleman's all-purpose name for German white wines in honour of the Hochheimer Königin-Victoria-Berg.

With that knowledge behind you, you can make your choice with the confidence that in matters of wine all you need is your own tongue and palate. There are no gaffes, just different tastes. The Germans have long drunk white wines with fish and meat alike and

it's only in a few snobbish places that wine waiters may try to impose a French red wine to drink with your steak. Resist. Drink the wine of the country. If you must have red, stick to Assmannshausen—or Ingelheim at a pinch. Or ignore this advice entirely and drink whatever you like.

You may also be pleased to find that you don't have to order a meal with your wine or even a whole bottle. In *Weinstuben*, *Weingärten*, *Keller* or

wherever, it's served by the glass, by the quarter- and half-litre in open carafes and at any time of day.

Other Beverages

With so many good wines flowing, the **beer** in the Rhineland doesn't get a lot of publicity, but it does get a lot of drinking. Mainz has a very good brew and the Munich and Dortmund brands are of course available. You can get excellent cider *(Apfelwein)* in Trier and it's not too bad in the Taunus.

Schnaps ought properly to refer only to Dutch gin, but the Germans have taken it over as a name for any hard, clear alcohol made from corn, barley, juniper or any other grain or berry that will distill into something to warm the cockles of your heart. Germans like to drink *Schnaps* in a shot-glass along with a glass of beer.

If you just want to be refreshed rather than stimulated, you'll find an unusually wide assortment of fruit **juices**, the best being *Johannisbeersaft* (red or black currant), *Apfelsaft* (apple) and *Traubensaft* (grape—non-alcoholic). In these days of health-conscious dieting there's a full gamut of mineral waters, with and without bubbles.

To Help You Order

Could we have a table?	**Ich hätte gerne einen Tisch.**
Waiter/waitress, please!	**Ober/Fräulein, bitte.**
The check, please.	**Zahlen, bitte.**

I would like...		**Ich möchte gerne...**	
beer	**ein Bier**	menu	**die Karte**
bread	**etwas Brot**	milk	**Milch**
butter	**etwas Butter**	mineral water	**Mineralwasser**
cheese	**Käse**	mustard	**etwas Senf**
coffee	**einen Kaffee**	potatoes	**Kartoffeln**
cold cuts	**Aufschnitt**	saccharin	**Süssstoff**
dessert	**eine Nachspeise**	salad	**Salat**
eggs	**Eier**	salt	**Salz**
fish	**Fisch**	soup	**eine Suppe**
fruit	**Obst**	sugar	**Zucker**
hors d'œuvre	**eine Vorspeise**	tea	**einen Tee**
ice-cream	**Eiskrem**	vegetables	**Gemüse**
lemon	**Zitrone**	whipped cream	**Schlagsahne**
meat	**Fleisch**	wine	**Wein**

...and Read the Menu

Apfel	apple	**Lamm**	lamb
Blumenkohl	cauliflower	**Leber**	liver
Bohnen	green beans	**Nierchen**	kidneys
Braten	roast beef	**Nudeln**	noodles
Ente	duck	**Pilze**	mushrooms
Erdbeeren	strawberries	**Reis**	rice
Forelle	trout	**Rindfleisch**	beef
Gurkensalat	cucumber salad	**Rippchen**	smoked pork chops
Hühnchen	chicken		
Jägerschnitzel	cutlet with mushroom sauce	**Rollmops**	marinated herring
Kalbfleisch	veal	**Sauerbraten**	pot roast
Klösse	dumplings	**Schinken**	ham
Kohl	cabbage	**Schweinefleisch**	pork
Kraftbrühe	bouillon	**Spargel**	asparagus
Kuchen	cake	**Wild**	game
Wurst	sausage		
100 **Lachs**	salmon	**Zwiebeln**	onions

How to Get There

Although the fares and conditions described below have all been carefully checked, it is advisable to consult a travel agent for the latest information on fares and other arrangements.

From Great Britain

BY AIR: Besides first class and economy, special weekend excursion fares are also available. As the name implies, you must travel both ways on a weekend; maximum stay is one month. There are daily flights from London to Düsseldorf, Cologne and Frankfurt. Weekend fares also exist on flights from Manchester and Birmingham to Düsseldorf. Special reductions are possible for spouse, children, young people and students, school and other affiliated groups.

Charter Flights and Package Tours: Most tour operators use surface transport to the Rhine Valley, but there are a few packages featuring air passage. You can choose between Rhine cruises, with lodging and excursions, and two-centre holidays. Special group fares on scheduled airlines (organized by travel agents) or charter flights would save you money. There are also some very cheap package holidays, with or without accommodation.

BY RAIL: The most direct route is via Dover and Ostend, fastest trains being the Tauern express and the Ostend-Vienna express, for which you must reserve seats. The trip takes around 11 hours. You might consider night travel, cheaper than the ordinary round-trip ticket, or look into special fares for students, young people and senior citizens. European Money Spinner Fares, available from the U.K. to ten German destinations, offer large discounts on round-trip tickets. Within Germany, "Tourist Cards" entitle the bearer to 9–16 days unlimited travel, and the Inter-Rail card is, of course, valid. Children under 12 are eligible for reductions on all fares. See page 123 for further information on reduced-price train tickets.

BY COACH: Europabus services connect London and Cologne all year long, though there are more departures during the summer. The London–Cologne trip takes about 12 hours; Cologne–London, slightly longer.

BY CAR: The quickest Channel crossing is Dover to Ostend. Travellers from the north could take advantage of Hull–Rotterdam. The main route goes from Ostend through Brussels to Cologne.

BY BOAT: Major cities on the Rhine and its tributaries (such as Amsterdam, Rotterdam, Basel) offer cruises to and from the Rhineland. There are fare reductions for children and special groups. Some tour operators will fly you out from London to board in Holland.

From North America

BY AIR: Non-stop flights leave daily from dozens of major cities in the U.S. and Canada for Frankfurt and Düsseldorf, some with connecting service to Cologne. Direct, daily flights link New York and Cologne.

Various reduced-price tickets, such as the Excursion Fare and the APEX (Advance Purchase Excursion) Fare, are available. The Excursion Fare, valid for a period of 14 to 60 days, requires no advance booking. The APEX Fare must be reserved 30 days prior to departure and is offered for periods of 14 to 60 days.

Charter Flights and Package Tours: A number of packages are available featuring Rhine cruises. The traveller may use the ship as hotel and go ashore each day for sightseeing expeditions. Meals and cabin accommodation are included; onshore sightseeing tours are extra. The other possibility is to combine hotel stays with a variety of river and land excursions.

Visitors from outside Europe may travel on the Eurailpass, a flat-rate unlimited mileage ticket, valid for first-class rail travel anywhere in Western Europe outside Great Britain. Eurail Youthpass offers second-class travel at a cheaper rate to anyone under 26.

When to Go

The best months for cruising on the Rhine are April–June and September–October, when the weather is pleasant and fewer tourists crowd the steamers. The year-round climate is generally mild, though you should expect rain at any time. The banks of the Rhine are at their most beautiful in the fall, when the vineyards turn to gold.

Average monthly (day-time) temperatures:

	J	F	M	A	M	J	J	A	S	O	N	D
°F	37	41	52	61	68	73	77	75	70	57	46	39
°C	3	5	11	16	20	23	25	24	21	14	8	4

Planning Your Budget

To give you an idea of what to expect, here's a list of average prices in marks (DM). They can only be approximate, however, as even in West Germany inflation creeps relentlessly up.

Airport transfers. Cologne-Bonn: bus to city centres DM 5, taxi to Bonn DM 35, to Cologne DM 25. Düsseldorf: train DM 2, taxi DM 7. Frankfurt: train DM 1.50, taxi DM 25.

Babysitters. DM 7 to 10 per hour.

Bicycle hire. DM 8 per day, DM 4 per day with railway ticket.

Camping. DM 5 to 12 for two persons with car and tent or caravan (trailer).

Car hire. VW Polo DM 38 per day, DM 0.30 per km., DM 385 for weekly unlimited mileage. Audi 100 LS DM 66 per day, DM 0.55 per km., DM 720 for weekly unlimited mileage. Mercedes 200/230 Automatic DM 86 per day, DM 0.80 per km., DM 1,100 for weekly unlimited mileage. 12% VAT and third-party insurance included; full insurance coverage DM 12 extra per day.

Cigarettes. DM 2.50 to 3 per packet of 20.

Entertainment. Cinema DM 8 to 10, theatre DM 10 to 50, discotheque DM 15 to 20 (first drink included), nightclub DM 20 to 40 (first drink included).

Hairdressers. Man's haircut DM 7 to 15, woman's haircut DM 8 to 15, shampoo and set DM 12 to 25, blow-dry DM 10 to 20, colour rinse DM 10 to 15.

Hotels. Double room with breakfast per night: in hotels DM 60 to 200, in inns and boarding houses DM 40 to 90, in private houses DM 25 to 50. Add DM 30 per day for full board.

Meals and drinks. Continental breakfast DM 6 to 8, lunch or dinner in fairly good establishment DM 20, wine ($\frac{1}{2}$-litre carafe) from DM 4, bottle of wine from DM 8, beer ($\frac{1}{2}$ l.) DM 2, coffee DM 2 to 3.50.

River cruises. Cologne–Mainz (direct) DM 95, Koblenz–Mainz DM 40, Koblenz–Trier (2 days) DM 80.

Taxis. Meter starts at DM 3, plus DM 1.40 per km.

Trains. Bonn–Frankfurt (2nd-class, one way) DM 25, Frankfurt–Heidelberg DM 14.

BLUEPRINT for a Perfect Trip

An A-Z Summary of Practical Information and Facts

Contents

Airports
Babysitters
Bicycle Hire
Camping
Car Hire
Cigarettes, Cigars, Tobacco
Clothing
Communications (post offices, mail, telegrams, telephone)
Complaints
Consulates
Converter Charts
Customs and Entry Formalities
Driving in Germany
Electric Current
Emergencies
Guides and Tours
Hairdressers
Health and Medical Care
Hiking
Hitch-hiking
Hotels and Accommodation

Hours
Language
Laundry and Dry-cleaning
Maps
Money Matters (currency, banking hours, credit cards, traveller's cheques)
Newspapers and Magazines
Photography
Police
Public Holidays
Radio and TV
Religious Services
River Cruises
Spas and Health Resorts
Time Differences
Toilets
Tourist Information Offices
Transport (buses, taxis, trains, Europabus)
Youth Hostels
Some Useful Expressions

AIRPORTS* *(Flughafen).* Three major airports serve the Rhineland: Düsseldorf, Cologne-Bonn and Frankfurt. All three handle international flights. The terminals are modern—some of the most efficient in Europe—with restaurants, snack bars, news- and souvenir-stands, hotel-reservation desks, banks, post offices, duty-free shops, etc. The airport information offices are normally open from 6 a.m. to 10 p.m.

Buses or direct trains (in addition to taxis) circulate between the airport and the respective city centres.

Düsseldorf. The Düsseldorf-Lohausen Airport is 11 kilometres from the city centre. The urban train *(S-Bahn),* an extension of the city's underground system *(U-Bahn),* operates between the airport and the main railway station every half hour from about 5 a.m. to 11 p.m., taking around 20 minutes.

Cologne-Bonn. The Köln-Bonn Airport at Wahn on the right bank of the Rhine lies 14 kilometres from Cologne, 16 kilometres from Bonn. Buses leave from the airport for Cologne's main railway station and for its Köln-Deutz station on the right bank every 20 minutes and for Bonn's main railway station every 30 minutes. The trips take 20 to 30 minutes.

Frankfurt. It is 10 kilometres from the Rhein-Main Airport to the main railway station. A train leaves every 20 minutes for the quarter-hour trip. Tickets must be bought from blue vending machines before boarding the train. Frankfurt's airport, the country's main gateway, has frequent connections to all domestic airports.

Lufthansa (Germany's national airline) reservation desks can be reached by calling:

Bonn, tel. (02221) 5195   Düsseldorf, tel. (0211) 8885
Cologne, tel. (0221) 20788   Frankfurt, tel. (0611) 230521

A

| Where's the bus/train to…? | **Wo steht der Bus/der Zug nach…?** |
| What time does it leave? | **Wann fährt er ab?** |

B

BABYSITTERS*. Most hotels will organize a sitter, but this may consist of no more than someone looking in periodically. If you want a person on hand throughout your absence, you should call, or have the hotel receptionist call, a nearby university for a list of students available for babysitting.

| Can you get me a babysitter for tonight/tomorrow evening? | **Können Sie mir für heute abend/ morgen abend einen Babysitter besorgen?** |

BICYCLE HIRE* *(Fahrradverleih)*. Discovering the beauty of the Rhineland by bicycle is a delightful experience, and it's possible to hire a bike in many towns. From April until the end of October, you can hire one at a railway station and return it to another station dealing with vehicle rental; railway-users get a special discount, and tours will be suggested if you wish. Inquire at any station or tourist office.

| Are there bicycles for hire at this station? | **Kann man an diesem Bahnhof Fahrräder mieten?** |

C

CAMPING*. Camping is highly developed in Germany. Sites, usually open from May to September, are indicated by the international blue sign with a black tent on a white background. Tourist offices give out a free map-folder with full details on campsites throughout the Rhineland. The German Automobile Club ADAC and the German Camping Club (DCC) also publish camping guides.

If you camp off the beaten track, be sure to obtain the permission of the proprietor or the police, and note that camping in the rest-areas off the motorways is not permitted.

May we camp here?	**Dürfen wir hier zelten?**
Is there a campsite near here?	**Gibt es in der Nähe einen Zelt- platz?**
Do you have room for a tent/ caravan (trailer)?	**Haben Sie Platz für ein Zelt/ einen Wohnwagen?**

CAR HIRE*. See also DRIVING. Consult your hotel receptionist or
the yellow pages of the telephone book under "Autovermietung" for

addresses of leading car hire firms. Rentals can also be arranged at the airports and railway stations. Firms offer a full range of German cars. You'll need a valid driving licence to hire a car; the minimum age is 21. Normally a deposit is charged, but holders of major credit cards are exempt.

Special weekend and weekly unlimited mileage rates are often available. It is usually possible to have the car delivered to the hotel. Major firms allow you to turn the vehicle in at another point (without any extra charge if it's within Germany).

Many airlines arrange fly/drive holidays, and the German Federal Railways has a "Rail-and-Road" car hire system in more than 40 towns.

CIGARETTES, CIGARS, TOBACCO* *(Zigaretten, Zigarren, Tabak).* Foreign cigarette brands (under German licence) and a wide range of cigars and tobacco are sold in specialized tobacco shops, at kiosks and in cigarette machines. Most domestic brands *(Ernte 23, HB, Astor)* resemble American cigarettes, but there are others with coarser tobacco. When buying cigarettes at street vending machines, the small change is returned in the packet.

A packet of.../A box of matches, please.	**Eine Schachtel.../Streichhölzer, bitte.**

CLOTHING. Temperatures are rarely extreme in the Rhineland, which means that year-round climate is generally mild. In winter, warm but not cumbersome clothing is what's needed. In spring and autumn, replace the winter coat by a raincoat. In summer it may also rain, so don't forget an umbrella, and pack a sweater, too.

At better hotels and restaurants, more formal clothes are expected, but there are few places where a tie is obligatory.

COMMUNICATIONS

Post offices of Germany's Bundespost are generally open from 8 a.m. to 6 p.m., Monday to Friday, till 12 noon on Saturdays. They also handle telegrams and telephone calls. Post offices at main railway stations in larger towns are open till late in the evening on weekdays. Mail boxes are painted yellow with a black post-horn.

Poste restante (general delivery). This service is taken care of by the town's central post office. Have mail addressed to you c/o *Hauptpost-* **107**

C *lagernd,* and take your passport or identity card when you go to pick it up.

Some main post offices:

Münsterplatz 17, D-5300 Bonn
An den Dominikanern, D-5000 Köln
Hauptbahnhof, D-5400 Koblenz
Bahnhofstrasse 2, D-6500 Mainz

Telegrams. In Germany, telegrams are handled by the post offices, but cables can also be phoned in from hotels or private phones.

Telephone. Telephone booths, glass boxes with yellow frames, bear a sign with a black receiver in a yellow square. Calls within Germany can be dialled direct from any public telephone box. Area code numbers are listed next to the town name in the phone book. Calls abroad can be made from booths with a green disc marked *Ausland.* Communications are cheaper between 6 and 10 p.m., and cheaper still between 10 p.m. and 6 a.m., as well as on Sundays and holidays. Hotels are authorized to ask a small charge for calls placed.

Some useful numbers:

Inquiries, domestic, 118, international, 00 118
Operator, domestic, 0 10, international, 00 10

Where's the (nearest) post office?	**Wo ist das (nächste) Postamt?**
A stamp for this letter/postcard, please.	**Eine Briefmarke für diesen Brief/ diese Karte, bitte.**
express (special delivery)	**Eilzustellung**
airmail	**Luftpost**
registered	**Eingeschrieben**
Have you received any mail for…?	**Ist Post da für…?**
I want to send a telegram to…	**Ich möchte ein Telegramm nach… aufgeben.**
Can I use the telephone?	**Kann ich das Telefon benutzen?**
Can you get me this number in…?	**Können Sie mich mit dieser Nummer in … verbinden?**
reverse-charge (collect) call	**R-Gespräch**
personal (person-to-person) call	**Gespräch mit Voranmeldung**

COMPLAINTS. If something goes wrong that you cannot take care of
108 yourself, report the matter to the local tourist office.

In hotels, restaurants and shops, complaints should be made to the proprietor or manager. If you fail to obtain on-the-spot satisfaction in the case of a justifiable and serious complaint, contact the Deutscher Hotel- und Gaststättenverband:

Kronprinzenstrasse 46, 5300 Bonn; tel. (02221) 36 20 16/18/19

Department stores have a customers' counter *(Kundendienst)* for any problems.

CONSULATES *(Konsulat)*

Canada	Michaelplatz, 5300 Bonn; tel. (02221) 35 10 41
Eire	Godesberger Allee 119, 5300 Bonn; tel. (02221) 37 69 37/38/39
United Kingdom	Friedrich-Ebert-Allee 77, 5300 Bonn; tel. (02221) 23 40 61 (chancellery)
	Bockenheimer Landstrasse 51–53, 6000 Frankfurt am Main; tel. (0611) 72 04 06/09
U.S.A.	Deichmanns Aue, 5300 Bonn; tel. (02221) 89 32 82
	Siesmayerstrasse 21, 6000 Frankfurt am Main; tel. (0611) 74 00 71

CONVERTER CHARTS. For fluid measures, see page 112. West Germany uses the metric system.

Temperature

Distance

Weight

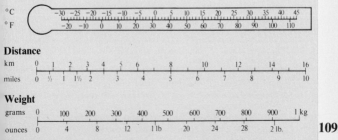

C **CUSTOMS** *(Zoll)* **and ENTRY FORMALITIES.** For a stay of up to three months, a valid passport is sufficient for citizens of Australia, Canada, New Zealand, South Africa and U.S.A. Visitors from Eire and the United Kingdom need only an identity card to enter West Germany.

In recent years, German customs officials have become more thorough, but they are unlikely to quibble over details. Here's what you can take into West Germany duty free and, when returning home, into your own country:

Entering West Germany from:	Cigarettes	Cigars	Tobacco	Spirits	Wine
1)	200 or	50 or	250 g.	1 l. and	2 l.
2)	300 or	75 or	400 g.	1.5 l. and	3 l.
3)	400 or	100 or	500 g.	1 l. and	2 l.
Into:					
Canada	200 and	50 and	900 g.	1.1 l. or	1.1 l.
Eire	200 or	50 or	250 g.	1 l. and	2 l.
U.K.	200 or	50 or	250 g.	1 l. and	2 l.
U.S.A.	200 and	100 and	4)	1 l. or	1 l.

1) EEC countries with goods bought tax free, and other European countries
2) EEC countries with goods not bought tax free
3) countries outside Europe
4) a reasonable quantity

Items and equipment for personal use may be brought in without any problem.

Currency restrictions. There are no restrictions on the import or export of marks or any other currency.

I've nothing to declare.	**Ich habe nichts zu verzollen.**
It's for personal use.	**Es ist für meinen persönlichen Gebrauch bestimmt.**
It's a present.	**Das ist ein Geschenk.**

DRIVING IN GERMANY

Entering Germany. To bring your car into Germany you will need:

- a national (or international for those coming from the U.S.A., Australia, South Africa) driving licence
- car registration papers
- a national identity sticker for your car and a red warning triangle in case of breakdown, as well as a first-aid kit

Insurance. Third-party insurance is compulsory. Visitors from abroad, except those from EEC and certain other European countries, will have to present their international insurance certificate (Green Card) or take out third-party insurance at the German border. Seatbelts are obligatory, and if you don't wear them insurance companies reduce compensation in case of accidents.

Driving conditions. Drive on the right, pass on the left. Traffic in Germany follows the same basic rules that apply in most countries, but some may differ:

- on the *Autobahn* (motorway, expressway): 1) passing another vehicle on the right is prohibited; 2) on certain stretches (watch for signs) cars with caravans (trailers) are not allowed to overtake; 3) in a traffic jam *(Stau)*, cars in the right lane must keep close to the right, those in the left lane close to the left, to allow police or emergency vehicles to pass in the middle
- in the absence of traffic lights, stop or yield signs, vehicles coming from the right have priority at intersections, unless otherwise indicated
- at roundabouts (traffic circles), approaching cars must give way to traffic already in mid-stream, unless otherwise indicated
- trams must be passed on the right and never at a stop (unless there's a traffic island)
- at dusk, and in case of bad visibility, headlights or dipped headlights must be used; driving with parking lights only is forbidden, even in built-up areas

Speed limits. The speed limit is 100 kilometres per hour (62 mph) on all open roads except for motorways and dual carriageways (divided highways), where there's no limit unless otherwise indicated. In town, speed is restricted to 50 kph (31 mph). Cars towing caravans may not exceed 80 kph (50 mph).

D

Traffic police (see also POLICE) may confiscate the car keys of persons they consider unfit to drive. Drinking and driving, for example, is a very serious offence in Germany. The permissible alcohol level in the blood is 0.8 per mille (millilitres), or about two glasses of beer. Be careful, too, to stay within speed limits; the police are getting more and more strict, and traffic radar is used both inside and outside of towns.

Breakdowns. In the event of a breakdown on the *Autobahn* and other important roads, use one of the emergency telephones located every second kilometre (the nearest one is indicated by a small arrow on the reflector poles at the roadside). Ask for *Strassenwachthilfe*, a service run jointly by the German automobile clubs ADAC *(Allgemeiner Deutscher Automobil Club)* and AvD *(Automobilclub von Deutschland)*. Assistance is free, only spare parts have to be paid for.

Fuel and oil *(Benzin; Öl)*. You'll find service stations everywhere, many of them self-service. It's customary to tip attendants for any extra attention.

Fluid measures

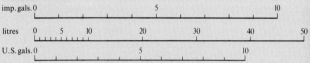

Road signs. Most road signs employed in West Germany are international pictographs, but here are some written ones you might come across:

Einbahnstrasse	One-way street
Einordnen	Get in lane
Fussgänger	Pedestrians
Kurzparkzone	Short-term parking
Links fahren	Keep left
Parken verboten	No parking
Schlechte Fahrbahn	Bad road surface
Strassenarbeiten	Road works (Men working)
Umleitung	Diversion (Detour)
Vorsicht	Caution

(International) Driving Licence	**(Internationaler) Führerschein**
Car Registration Papers	**Kraftfahrzeugpapiere**
Green Card	**Grüne Karte**

Where's the nearest car park?	**Wo ist der nächste Parkplatz?**
Are we on the right road for…?	**Sind wir auf der richtigen Strasse nach…?**
Fill the tank, please.	**Bitte volltanken.**
Check the oil/tires/battery, please.	**Kontrollieren Sie bitte das Öl/ die Reifen/die Batterie.**
I've had a breakdown.	**Ich habe eine Panne.**
There's been an accident.	**Es ist ein Unfall passiert.**

ELECTRIC CURRENT. West Germany has 220–250-volt, 50-cycle AC. **E**

EMERGENCIES. See also under CONSULATES, HEALTH AND MEDICAL CARE or POLICE according to the type of emergency.

The emergency numbers below cover the whole country. Others are listed on the first pages of local telephone directories. If you don't speak German, try English or ask the first person you see to help you call.

Police	110
Fire, first aid, ambulance	112

These words are handy to know in difficult situations:

Fire	**Feuer**
Help	**Hilfe**
Police	**Polizei**
Stop	**Halt**
Please, can you place an emergency call for me to the…?	**Würden Sie bitte… für mich anrufen?**
police/fire brigade/hospital	**die Polizei/die Feuerwehr/ das Krankenhaus**

GUIDES and TOURS. See also RIVER CRUISES. Local tourist offices can put you in touch with qualified official guides and interpreters if you want a personally conducted tour or linguistic assistance. **G**

Most organized city tours start at the tourist offices. Longer guided bus tours run from all the major towns (Düsseldorf, Cologne, Bonn, Koblenz, Mainz) up and down the Rhine Valley to wine villages and other points of interest. Tourist offices have the details.

HAIRDRESSERS *(Damenfriseur)* **and BARBERS** *(Herrenfriseur)*⋆. In general, there is no problem in getting your hair done whenever and however you want. Rates range from *haute coiffure* levels in the centres of Cologne, Bonn, Düsseldorf and Mainz to very reasonable ones in smaller towns and villages and are usually displayed in the window. Although most establishments are open on Saturdays and closed on Mondays, there may be some local variations.

For tipping suggestions, see inside back cover.

I'd like a shampoo and set.	**Waschen und Legen, bitte.**
haircut	**Schneiden**
shave	**Rasieren**
blow-dry (brushing)	**mit dem Fön trocknen**
colour rinse	**eine Farbspülung**
Don't cut it too short.	**Schneiden Sie es nicht zu kurz.**
A little more off (here).	**(Hier) etwas kürzer.**

HEALTH and MEDICAL CARE. Ask your insurance company before leaving home if medical treatment in Germany is covered. Visitors whose insurance does not reimburse medical bills abroad can take out a short-term holiday policy before setting forth. Citizens of EEC countries may also use the German Health Services for medical treatment. Ask for the leaflet SA 28 and the CM 1 application form at your local Health and Social Security Office.

In the event of accident or serious illness, call the Red Cross *(Rotes Kreuz)*, or the medical emergency service, *Ärztlicher Notdienst* (telephone number in the local directory), which will give you doctors' addresses.

It is perfectly safe to drink the tap water in West Germany; only rarely will you see the sign *Kein Trinkwasser*.

Pharmacies are open during normal shopping hours. At night and on Sundays and holidays, all chemists' shops display the address of the nearest one open.

Where's the nearest (all-night) pharmacy?	**Wo ist die nächste (Dienst-) Apotheke?**
I need a doctor/dentist.	**Ich brauche einen Arzt/Zahnarzt.**
I have a pain here.	**Ich habe hier Schmerzen.**
stomach ache	**Magenschmerzen**
headache	**Kopfschmerzen**
a fever	**Fieber**

114

HIKING. Germany may be better known for its industry than its parks, but the country still has a great deal to offer the hiker and nature lover (see also under MAPS).

The following organization can give you information about the possibilities: Verband Deutscher Gebirgs- und Wandervereine,

Hospitalstrasse 21B, D-7000 Stuttgart; tel. (0711) 29 53 36,

or, for younger enthusiasts: Deutsche Wanderjugend,

Herbergstrasse 11, D-7000 Stuttgart; tel. (0711) 46 60 05.

HITCH-HIKING. There's nothing actually to discourage hitch-hiking, but there's little to encourage it either: you'll be lucky if anyone stops for you. Only on the *Autobahn* or its access roads is it illegal. Student associations (at the universities) can often arrange for inter-city trips *(Mitfahrgelegenheit).*

HOTELS and ACCOMMODATION*. See also CAMPING and YOUTH HOSTELS. Local tourist offices publish lists annually with full details on classifications, amenities and prices of accommodation. The *German Hotel Guide,* distributed free by the German National Tourist Office in your country, also offers a good selection. During the summer, weekends and periods with special events, it is advisable to book ahead. The Allgemeine Deutsche Zimmerreservierung (ADZ) operates a computer reservation system at:

Beethovenstrasse 61, D-6000 Frankfurt am Main; tel. (0611) 74 07 67.

If you are touring by car and only spending a night or so in any one place, look out for *Zimmer frei* ("room to let") signs along the way.

Other types of accommodation are available in castles, mansions and historic hostelries. Information and a booklet on staying in castles, *Gast im Schloss,* can be obtained from tourist offices, local travel agencies or from the association:

Gast im Schloss, Vor der Burg 10, D-3526 Trendelburg.

Holiday flats (apartments) and bungalows of all sorts can be rented in the Rhine Valley. A list of inclusive tours to Germany, published by the National Tourist Office, contains details.

Farmhouse holidays in Germany are described in a booklet called *Ferien auf dem Lande,* obtainable from:

Landschriften-Verlag, Kurfürstenstrasse 53, D-5300 Bonn.

H I'd like a single/double room. **Ich hätte gern ein Einzelzimmer/ein Doppelzimmer.**

with bath/shower **mit Bad/Dusche**

What's the rate per night/week? **Wieviel kostet es pro Nacht/Woche?**

HOURS. See also under COMMUNICATIONS, HEALTH AND MEDICAL CARE and MONEY MATTERS.

Museum hours vary, but are usually from 9 a.m. to 4 p.m.

Restaurant meals. Breakfast is served until 10 a.m., lunch from 12 noon to 2 p.m. and dinner from 6 to 9.30 p.m.

Shops are generally open from 9 a.m. to 6.30 p.m., Monday to Friday, till 2 p.m. on Saturdays (until 6 p.m. on the first Saturday of the month). Shops outside city centres usually close from 1 to 3 p.m.

Travel agencies operate from 9 a.m. to 6 p.m., Monday to Friday, till 12 noon on Saturdays.

L **LANGUAGE.** The German spoken in the Rhineland is melodious, though sometimes difficult to understand. English is widely understood and spoken, but don't take it for granted.

If you'd like to participate in a language course, you should get in touch with the Goethe-Institut, Referat 31 (Sprachkurse)

Lenbachplatz 3, D-8000 München

which offers language courses in the charming wine village of Boppard.

When entering a shop, it's customary to say *Guten Tag* (Good day) or *Guten Abend* (Good evening), and, of course, *Auf Wiedersehen* (Goodbye) when leaving. However, you will often hear the less formal *Tschö (Tschüs* elsewhere in Germany), simply meaning "Bye" or "See you soon".

The Berlitz phrase book GERMAN FOR TRAVELLERS covers most situations you are likely to encounter in Germany, and the German-English/English-German pocket dictionary contains a special menu-reader supplement.

Do you speak English? **Sprechen Sie Englisch?**

I'm sorry, I don't speak German. **Leider spreche ich nicht Deutsch.**

LAUNDRY and DRY-CLEANING. Having your laundry washed or cleaned by the hotel is of course the quickest and most convenient method, but prices are correspondingly high; it is therefore worth seeking out a neighbourhood dry-cleaners or a laundromat *(Waschsalon)*.

Where's the nearest laundry/ dry-cleaners?	**Wo ist die nächste Wäscherei/ Reinigung?**

MAPS. News-stands and bookshops sell a large selection of maps of the Rhineland, but you get excellent free maps of cities and surrounding areas from the German National Tourist Office in your country, or, in Germany, at local tourist offices, hotels and car hire firms. Falk-Verlag, Hamburg, who prepared the maps for this book, have practical city maps of Bonn, Cologne, Düsseldorf, Frankfurt, Trier and Wiesbaden-Mainz, as well as general maps of Germany *(Der Grosse Autoatlas der Bundesrepublik)* and conveniently folded maps of the Rhine and Mosel areas *(Rund um Rhein und Ruhr* and *Rund um Saar und Mosel)*. For the hiker, there is a series called *Kompass Wanderkarten*—available in most bookstores—that will keep you on the right track.

I'd like a map/road map of this region.	**Ich möchte eine Landkarte/ Strassenkarte dieser Gegend.**
a street plan of...	**einen Stadtplan von...**

MONEY MATTERS

Currency. Germany's monetary unit is the *Deutsche Mark (DM)*. The mark is divided into 100 *Pfennig (Pf.)*.

   Coins: 1, 2, 5, 10 and 50 Pf. and DM 1, 2 and 5.
   Notes: DM 5, 10, 20, 50, 100, 500 and 1,000.

Banking hours are usually from 8.30 a.m. to 1 p.m. and 2.30 to 4 p.m., Monday to Friday (Thursday until 5.30 p.m.).

Changing money. Foreign currency can be changed in ordinary banks *(Bank)* and savings banks *(Sparkasse)*. It can also be done at travel agencies and hotels, but the exchange rates are not as good. The same is true of currency and traveller's cheques changed in shops or restaurants. If you need to change money outside banking hours, the main railway stations in larger towns have exchange offices *(Wechselstube)* open from early in the morning till late in the evening and on weekends.

M **Credit cards and traveller's cheques.** Traveller's cheques are welcome almost anywhere, and most major hotels and many restaurants and shops accept credit cards. Eurocheques are widely used in West Germany.

I want to change some pounds/dollars.	**Ich möchte Pfund/Dollars wechseln.**
Do you accept traveller's cheques?	**Nehmen Sie Reiseschecks?**
Can I pay with this credit card?	**Kann ich mit dieser Kreditkarte zahlen?**

N **NEWSPAPERS and MAGAZINES** *(Zeitung; Zeitschrift).* Major British, American and Continental newspapers and magazines are on sale at news-stands in the city centres as well as at bigger hotels, at railway stations and airports.

A free guide to forthcoming events *(Rheinland Veranstaltungen)*, published twice a year, is available at tourist offices.

Have you any English-language newspapers?	**Haben Sie Zeitungen in englischer Sprache?**

P **PHOTOGRAPHY.** Some of the world's best cameras come from West Germany, so you might even think of getting equipped here. All makes of film are easily found and developed overnight if need be.

I'd like a roll of film for this camera.	**Ich hätte gern einen Film für diesen Apparat.**
black-and-white film	**Schwarzweissfilm**
colour prints	**Farbfilm**
colour slides	**Diafilm**
How long will it take to develop this film?	**Wie lange dauert das Entwickeln?**
May I take a picture (of you)?	**Darf ich (Sie) fotografieren?**

POLICE *(Polizei).* West Germany's police wear green uniforms. You'll see them on white motorcycles or in white-and-green cars.

Street parking in towns is supervised by policemen and -women in dark-blue uniforms (if you are fined, they have the right to ask you to pay on the spot).

The police emergency number is 110.

Where's the nearest police station? **Wo ist die nächste Polizeiwache?**

PUBLIC HOLIDAYS *(Feiertag)*. The chart below shows the public holidays celebrated in the Rhineland, when banks, official services and many restaurants are closed. If a holiday falls on a Thursday, many people make it into an extended weekend.

On December 24 (Christmas Eve), theatres and cinemas, concert halls, shops, restaurants and coffee houses close at midday.

January 1	*Neujahr*	New Year's Day
May 1	*Tag der Arbeit*	Labour Day
June 17	*Tag der Deutschen Einheit*	Day of National Unity
November 1	*Allerheiligen*	All Saints' Day
December 25	*Weihnacht*	Christmas
December 26	*Zweiter Weihnachtsfeiertag*	
movable dates:	*Karfreitag*	Good Friday
	Ostermontag	Easter Monday
	Himmelfahrt	Ascension Day
	Pfingstmontag	Whit Monday
	Fronleichnam	Corpus Christi
	Buss- und Bettag (3rd Wednesday in Nov.)	Day of Prayer and Repentance

Are you open tomorrow?　　　　**Haben Sie morgen offen?**

RADIO and TV *(Radio; Fernsehen)*. You can easily pick up the British Forces Broadcasting System (BFBS) or the American Forces Network (AFN) anywhere in the Rhineland. Short-wave reception is excellent, especially at night. German television broadcasts on three channels, two national—ARD (Channel One) and ZDF (Channel Two)—plus one regional third channel *(Drittes Programm)* provided by the ARD.

RELIGIOUS SERVICES. West Germans are divided almost equally between Protestants and Roman Catholics. The northern provinces tend to be predominantly Protestant, while the Rhineland and the south are mostly Catholic. Nevertheless in every town of the Rhine and Mosel regions there are Protestant churches; some (at Bad Godes-

R berg and Wiesbaden) hold services in English. Major cities have synagogues.

Is there a Protestant church/ synagogue (near) here?	**Gibt es hier (in der Nähe) eine evangelische Kirche/eine Synagoge?**
What time is mass/the service?	**Wann beginnt die Messe/der Gottesdienst?**

RIVER CRUISES*. Daily scheduled services on the Rhine and Mosel operate from April to the end of October. The choice of boats and trips is obviously best during high season (July-August).

Suppose you start in Cologne: the Köln-Düsseldorfer Deutsche Rheinschiffahrt AG (abbreviated KD) offers excursions on large and small motorboats, paddle-steamers and hydrofoils. The most popular tour, between Cologne and Mainz, has about 35 stops, and you get on or off wherever you like, even exchanging a return train ticket for a boat ticket at the KD stops. The classic two-day Mosel tour runs from Koblenz to Trier, with stops in all the wine-growing villages.

Boats are usually well equipped, with restaurants and snack bars and cabins for overnight journeys. The KD organizes special programmes on fixed dates, like music and dancing and children's parties, as well as excursions combined with sightseeing tours on land. The company also ships cars to save passengers the trouble of going back to pick them up.

If you want more detailed information, contact:

Köln-Düsseldorfer, Frankenwerft 15, D-5000 Köln; tel. (0221) 2 08 81.

Around Bonn, Cologne and Düsseldorf, smaller cruise companies offer shorter excursions. Check with the local tourist office for their addresses.

Where can I catch the boat?	**Wo nimmt man das Schiff?**
upstream/downstream	**flussaufwärts/flussabwärts**

S **SPAS and HEALTH RESORTS.** Officially recognized spas and health resorts offer recreational facilities as well as a variety of entertainment. A list of spas and health resorts in the Rhine Valley can be had from the Deutscher Bäderverband e.V.:

Schumannstrasse 111, D-5300 Bonn (tel. [02221] 21 10 88/89).

TIME DIFFERENCES. West Germany follows Greenwich Mean Time + 1, and in summer the clocks are put forward one hour.

Los Angeles	Chicago	New York	London	**West Germany**
3 a.m.	5 a.m.	6 a.m.	11 a.m.	**noon**

What time is it, please?   **Wieviel Uhr ist es, bitte?**

TOILETS. Public toilets are easily found: most museums, all restaurants, bars, coffee houses, large stores, airports and railway stations have facilities. If there's an attendant, and handtowels and soap are offered, you should leave a small tip. Always have several 10-Pfennig coins ready in case the door has a slot machine.

Toilets may be labelled with symbols of a man or a woman or the initials *W.C.* Otherwise *Herren* (Gentlemen) or *Damen* (Ladies) are indicated.

Where are the toilets, please?   **Wo sind die Toiletten, bitte?**

TOURIST INFORMATION OFFICES. The German National Tourist Board's—Deutsche Zentrale für Tourismus e.V. (DZT)—headquarters is at:

Beethovenstrasse 69, D-6000 Frankfurt am Main; tel. (0611) 75721

It maintains offices in many countries throughout the world:

Canada   P.O. Box 417, 2 Fundy, Place Bonaventure, Montreal, Que. H5A 1B8; tel. (514) 878-9885

United Kingdom 61, Conduit Street, London W1R OEN; tel. (01) 734-2600

U.S.A.   630 Fifth Avenue, New York, NY 10020; tel. (212) 757-8570

Broadway Plaza, Suite 1714, 700 South Flower Street, Los Angeles, CA 90017; tel..(213) 688-7332

104 South Michigan Avenue, Chicago, IL 60603; tel. (312) 263-2958

T Landesverkehrsverband Rheinland, a general tourist office for the Northern Rhineland, is located at:

Rheinallee 69, D-5300 Bonn-Bad Godesberg; tel. (02221) 362921

The Fremdenverkehrsverband Rheinland-Pfalz (Rhineland-Palatinate) is at:

Bahnhofstrasse 54–56, D-5400 Koblenz; tel. (0261) 35025

Here are the addresses of local tourist information offices in the bigger towns:

Bonn. Cassiusbastei; tel. (02221) 77466

Cologne. Beside the cathedral; tel. (0221) 2211

Düsseldorf. Konrad-Adenauer-Platz 12; tel. (0211) 350505

Frankfurt. Beethovenstrasse 61; tel. (0611) 752023

Koblenz. At the central railway station; tel. (0261) 31304

Mainz. Bahnhofsplatz 2; tel. (06131) 28371

Where's the tourist office? **Wo ist das Fremdenverkehrsamt?**

TRANSPORT (see also CAR HIRE and RIVER CRUISES)

City transport. Buses and trams both operate in larger towns. You buy your ticket from a vending machine or ticket kiosk at the bus/tram stop. Bonn, Düsseldorf, Frankfurt and (soon) Cologne, are also served by underground trains *(U-Bahn)*; the *U-Bahn* lines connecting with the suburbs are often called *S-Bahn*. Maps showing the various lines and stations are displayed outside every station. The *U-Bahn* usually runs from 5 a.m. to 1 a.m.

Inter-city bus services. Rural areas are served by the Federal Railways *(Bundesbahn)* buses and the Federal Post Office *(Bundespost)* buses, as well as by local companies. Bus terminals are invariably close to a railway station, and there you'll find information about routes and fares.

Taxis*. Taxis—be it in the villages or the big cities—abound, either roaming the streets or waiting at ranks (usually right beside the station). You can also phone for a taxi wherever you are; numbers are listed on a separate page in the front of phone books. All cabs have meters; drivers ask for a supplement for luggage carried in the trunk.

122 Tip about 10% of the fare.

Trains*. The Deutsche Bundesbahn (DB) trains are extremely comfortable and fast, as well as punctual. They are classified in the following categories:

TEE *(Trans-Europ-Express)*	The fastest train; with supplement; first class only.
IC *(Intercity)*	Long-distance inter-city trains; some only first, others with first and second class; with supplement.
DC *(City-D-Zug)*	Short-distance inter-city trains, with few stops at major points only; first and second class, with supplement on trips of less than 50 kilometres.
D *(Schnellzug)*	Also called *D-Zug*; intermediate- to long-distance trains.
E *(Eilzug)*	Trains making local stops.
Nahverkehrszug	Local trains, stop at all stations.

Tickets for distances of up to 50 kilometres are valid for two days, those over 50 kilometres, for two months. A number of special reduced-price offers and bargain tickets are available:

European Money-Spinner Fares offer return (round-trip) journeys from the U.K. to ten selected destinations within Germany at about 25% off.

DB Tourist Cards for foreign visitors only, through certain travel agencies. Bring along your passport when ordering. The holder can travel for nine or 16 consecutive days on the entire network of the Deutsche Bundesbahn, as well as on KD boats (see also RIVER CRUISES).

Eurailpasses are special rover tickets covering most of Western Europe. For non-European residents only, to be purchased before leaving home.

Inter-Rail ticket users must be under 26 or over 65; they can travel by rail throughout Europe (except U.K.) for one month.

Tourenkarten, regional rail rover tickets for a given area (such as the central Rhineland) are bought in Germany. They allow ten days' unlimited travel on rail services, with 50% reduction on buses; the only requirement is that your rail journey must have covered at least 200 kilometres one way *before* you can obtain it.

Children under 4 travel free, from 4 to 11 inclusive, half price.

For further details, ask for the brochure *Discover Germany by Rail* at travel agencies.

T   **Europabus.** This international bus network is operated jointly by several European railway systems through areas of special touristic interest; in Germany, the carrier is the Deutsche Touring-Gesellschaft:

Am Römerhof 17, D‑6000 Frankfurt am Main; tel. (0611) 79 03 1

Where's the (main) railway station/the bus stop?	**Wo ist der (Haupt-)Bahnhof/die Bushaltestelle?**
When's the next bus/train to…?	**Wann fährt der nächste Bus/Zug nach…?**
I want a ticket to…	**Ich möchte eine Fahrkarte nach…**
single (one-way)	**einfach**
return (round-trip)	**hin und zurück**
first/second class	**erste/zweite Klasse**
Will you tell me when to get off?	**Können Sie mir bitte sagen, wann ich aussteigen muss?**
Where can I get a taxi?	**Wo finde ich ein Taxi?**
What's the fare to…?	**Was kostet es bis…?**

Y   **YOUTH HOSTELS** *(Jugendherberge).* If you are planning to make extensive use of youth hostels during your stay in the Rhineland, contact your national association before departure to obtain an international membership card, or write to the German Youth Hostel Association *(Deutsches Jugendherbergswerk)*:

P. O. Box 220, Bülowstrasse 26, D‑4930 Detmold

DAYS   **DAYS OF THE WEEK**

Sunday	**Sonntag**	Thursday	**Donnerstag**
Monday	**Montag**	Friday	**Freitag**
Tuesday	**Dienstag**	Saturday	**Samstag**
Wednesday	**Mittwoch**		**(Sonnabend)**

NUMBERS

0	null	16	sechzehn
1	eins	17	siebzehn
2	zwei	18	achtzehn
3	drei	19	neunzehn
4	vier	20	zwanzig
5	fünf	21	einundzwanzig
6	sechs	30	dreissig
7	sieben	40	vierzig
8	acht	50	fünfzig
9	neun	60	sechzig
10	zehn	70	siebzig
11	elf	80	achtzig
12	zwölf	90	neunzig
13	dreizehn	100	(ein)hundert
14	vierzehn	101	hunderteins
15	fünfzehn	1000	(ein)tausend

SOME USEFUL EXPRESSIONS

yes/no	ja/nein
please/thank you	bitte/danke
excuse me/you're welcome	Entschuldigung/gern geschehen
how long/how far	wie lange/wie weit
where/when/how	wo/wann/wie
yesterday/today/tomorrow	gestern/heute/morgen
day/week/month/year	Tag/Woche/Monat/Jahr
left/right	links/rechts
big/small	gross/klein
cheap/expensive	billig/teuer
hot/cold	heiss/kalt
open/closed	offen/geschlossen
free (vacant)/occupied	frei/besetzt
I don't understand.	Ich verstehe nicht.
What does this mean?	Was bedeutet das?
Waiter/Waitress, please!	Ober/Fräulein, bitte!
How much is that?	Wieviel kostet das?

Index

An asterisk (*) next to a page number indicates a map reference. For index to Practical Information, see page 104.

Adenauer, Konrad 8, 25, 28
Assmannshausen 52*, 57

Bacharach 22, 52*, 54
Bad Godesberg 26, 30*, 46
Bad Homburg 30*, 62
Beethoven, Ludwig van 43, 44–45
Beilstein 31*, 68
Benrath, Schloss 82
Bernkastel-Kues 31*, 68
Bingen 52*, 54, 56
Bismarck, Otto von 25
Blücher, General 23, 57
Boat excursions 29, 32, 103, 120
Bonn 8, 28, 30*, 42*, 43–46
  Beethovenhaus 42*, 44
  Bundeshaus (parliament) 42*, 43
  Hofgarten 42*, 43
  Münster 42*, 46
  Museums
    Rheinisches Landes-museum 12, 42*, 45
    Städtisches Kunstmuseum 42*, 45
  Palais Schaumburg 42*, 43
  Poppelsdorfer Schloss 42*, 43
  Rathaus (Town Hall) 42*, 43
Boppard 52–53, 52*
Brentano, Clemens von 12
Brühl, Schloss 30*, 42–43

Burg (castle)
  ~ Eltz 31*, 68
  ~ Gutenfels 52*, 57
  ~ Katz 52*, 53
  ~ Maus 52*, 53
  ~ Pfalzgrafenstein 52*, 54, 57
  ~ Reichenstein 52*, 54, 57
  ~ Rheinfels 52*, 53
  ~ Rheinstein 52*, 54, 57
  ~ Sooneck 52*, 54
  ~ Stolzenfels 50, 51–52, 52*
Burgkmair, Hans 38

Camping 92, 103, 106
Carnival 8, 12, 89
Casinos 61, 91
Castles—see Burg and under town headings
Chamberlain, Neville 26, 46
Charlemagne 17
Churches—see under town headings
Cochem 31*, 68
Cologne (Köln) 8, 14–15, 22, 30*, 33–41, 39*, 89
  Altstadt (Old Town) 38, 84, 87
  Churches
    Antoniterkirche 39*, 40
    Madonna in den Trümmern 39*, 40
    St. Aposteln 39*, 40

Dom (cathedral) *33–36, 39**
Gürzenich *39*, 41*
Museums
    Ludwig *38*
    Römisch-Germanisches *15,*
    36–37, 39*
    Schnütgen *38, 39**
    Wallraf-Richartz *37, 39**
    Rathaus (Town Hall) *39*,*
    41
Concerts *90*
Cranach, Lucas *37, 61, 62*

Daun *31*, 76*
Dürer, Albrecht *37*
Düsseldorf *30*, 80–82*
    Altstadt (Old Town) *81*
    Hofgarten *81*
    Königsallee *81–82*
    Schloss Jägerhof *82*
    Städtisches Kunstmuseum
    81–82

Eau de Cologne *83*
Eberbach, Kloster *31*, 59–60*
Eckfeld *31*, 76*
Ehrenbreitstein (fortress) *48, 50,*
    52*
Eifel *11, 30*, 46, 75–76*
Eltville *31*, 58*
Esch *31*, 62*

Fireworks *90–91*
Fishing *92*
Food *92–95*
Frankfurt *30*, 62*
French *22–23, 24–25*

Geisenheim *52*, 58*
Görres, Joseph *23, 24*
Grosser Feldberg *31*, 62*
Gutenberg, Johannes *8, 19,*
    63–64, 66

Heidelberg *31*, 76–78, 90*
    Castle *76–77*
    Kurpfälzisches Museum *77*
    Philosophenweg *78*
    University *78*
Heine, Heinrich *11, 57, 58, 81*
Hiking *91, 115*
Hitler, Adolf *25–28, 46*
Holy Roman Empire *18–19, 23*
Hunsrück *11, 31*, 76*

Idarwald *31*, 76*
Idstein *31*, 62*

Jews *17–18, 23, 27, 79*
Johannisberg *52*, 58*

Kaub *52*, 54, 57*
Kings
    Friedrich Wilhelm IV *51, 52,*
    81
    Wilhelm I *25, 47*
Kleist, Heinrich von *62*
Koblenz *10, 46–50, 52*, 90*
    Alte Burg *48*
    Altstadt (Old Town) *48*
    Balduinbrücke *48*
    Deutsches Eck *10, 47*
    Kurfürstliches Schloss *47*
    Liebfrauenkirche *48*
    Metternich-Hof *48*
    Rheinanlagen *47*
    St. Kastor *47*
    Vier Türme *48*
Köln—see Cologne
Königstein *31*, 62*

Laacher See *30*, 46*
Language *28, 100, 116, 125*
Lieser (river) *31*, 75*
Limes Germanicus *15, 16*
Lochner, Stephan *36, 37, 62*
Lorch *52*, 57*

Lorelei   32, 52*, 53, 57, 58
Luther, Martin   15, 19, 79

Mainz   8, 17, 19, 22, 31*, 63–67, 63*, 89
  Dalberger Hof   63*, 67
  Dom (cathedral)   63*, 64–65
  Dommuseum   65
  Gutenberg Museum   63*, 66
  Marktbrunnen   63*, 66
Manderscheid   31*, 75, 76
Maria Laach (abbey)   46
Marienburg   68
Marx, Karl   24, 75
Mäuseturm   52*, 54, 56
Mazarin, Cardinal   22
Metternich, Prince Klemens von   24, 48, 58, 68
Mosel Valley   31*, 67–76
Mosenberg   76
Museums—see under town headings
Music   90

Napoleon   23, 48, 57, 81
Nassau, Johann von   20, 65
Nibelung legend   16, 80
Niederwald, Germania monument   52*, 56–57
Nightlife   87, 90–91, 103

Oberursel   31*, 62
Oberwesel   52*, 54
Oestrich-Winkel   52*, 58

Prehistoric man   12, 45, 77
Prussians   23–25

Religion   8, 15, 19–20
Rheingau   31*, 58–60, 96

Rhens   52, 52*
Rhine (Rhein)   10–11, 12, 29, 30*, 52* (see also Boat excursions)
Romans   13–16
Rüdesheim   52*, 56

St. Goar   52*, 53
St. Goarshausen   52*, 56, 57
Shopping   83–86
Speyer   31*, 78
Sports   91–92

Taunus   11, 31*, 61–62
Taunusstein   31*, 61–62
Thirty Years' War   21–22
Trains   32, 103, 123
Trier   15, 31*, 70–75
  Barbarathermen   74
  Dom (cathedral)   73
  Dreikönigenhaus   72
  Hauptmarkt   72
  Kaiserthermen   73–74
  Karl-Marx-Haus   75
  Landesmuseum   73
  Liebfrauenkirche   73
  Porta Nigra   71
  Simeonsstift   71

Verdun, Nikolaus von   35
Vineyards   52, 56
Volcanic lakes   46, 76

Wiesbaden   31*, 60–61
Wine   10, 56, 59–60, 67, 95–99
Worms   31*, 78–80
  Dom (cathedral)   78
  Lutherdenkmal   79
  Synagogue   79

Zell   31*, 68